CONFLICT IN THE 20th CENTURY

THE SECOND WORLD WAR

CHARLES MESSENGER

Edited by Dr John Pimlott

GALLERY BOOKS

An imprint of W.H. Smith Publishers Inc.
112 Madison Avenue
New York City 10016

INTRODUCTION

The Second World War is often described as a "total war." Although it began as a relatively restricted conflict between the Anglo-French allies and Germany over the political future of Poland in early September 1939, it gradually spread, drawing in country after country. In April 1940, Denmark and Norway were invaded by the Germans; a month later it was the turn of Belgium, the Netherlands, Luxemburg and France. Italy joined in on Germany's side in June and, after attacking British forces in Egypt and East Africa, took part in the invasion of Yugoslavia and Greece. In July 1941, Russia became involved as Axis forces – including units from Rumania and Hungary – poured across her borders in Operation Barbarossa. Five months later, Japan (at war with China since 1937) attacked American, British and Dutch possessions in the Far East to produce a truly global war. By 1945, campaigns had been fought in areas as far apart as the Atlantic and the Pacific and in climates as diverse as those of North Africa and Southeast Asia.

Totality also involved the political aims of the rival camps and the sacrifices made by them to achieve those aims. Both sides – Allied and Axis – fought to maintain their existing political structures while destroying those of their enemies and, in the process, diverted huge resources, human as well as material, to the pursuit of complete victory. At the same time, they fielded enormous armed forces on land, at sea and in the air, developed a whole generation of new, more devastating weapons and indulged in strategies which drew no distinction between civilian and military populations. Far more than in the First World War, conflict between 1939 and 1945 affected all aspects of human society.

By September 1945, when the Japanese finally accepted surrender, an estimated 50 million people had died and, with the atomic dust barely settled over Hiroshima and Nagasaki, a new, infinitely more dangerous era of history had dawned. In order to understand how the modern world has developed, the events of the six years of "total war" must be examined. That is the purpose of this volume.

DR JOHN PIMLOTT *Series Editor*

EDITORIAL PANEL

Series Editor:
Dr John Pimlott, Senior Lecturer in the Department of War Studies and International Affairs, RMA Sandhurst, UK

Editorial Advisory Panel:
Brigadier General James L Collins Jr, US Army Chief of Military History 1970–82

General Sir John Hackett, former Commander-in-Chief of the British Army of the Rhine and Principal of King's College, London, UK

Ian Hogg, retired Master Gunner of the Artillery, British Army, and editor of *Jane's Infantry Weapons*

John Keegan, former Senior Lecturer in the Department of War Studies and International Affairs, RMA Sandhurst, now Defense correspondent, *Daily Telegraph*

Professor Laurence Martin, Vice-Chancellor of the University of Newcastle-upon-Tyne, UK

The Author:
Charles Messenger retired from the British Army in 1980 to become a full-time military writer after 21 years' service in the Royal Tank Regiment. He has written a number of books and articles on defense and historical affairs.

German troops shelter behind a Panzer III, Russia, 1941.

CONTENTS

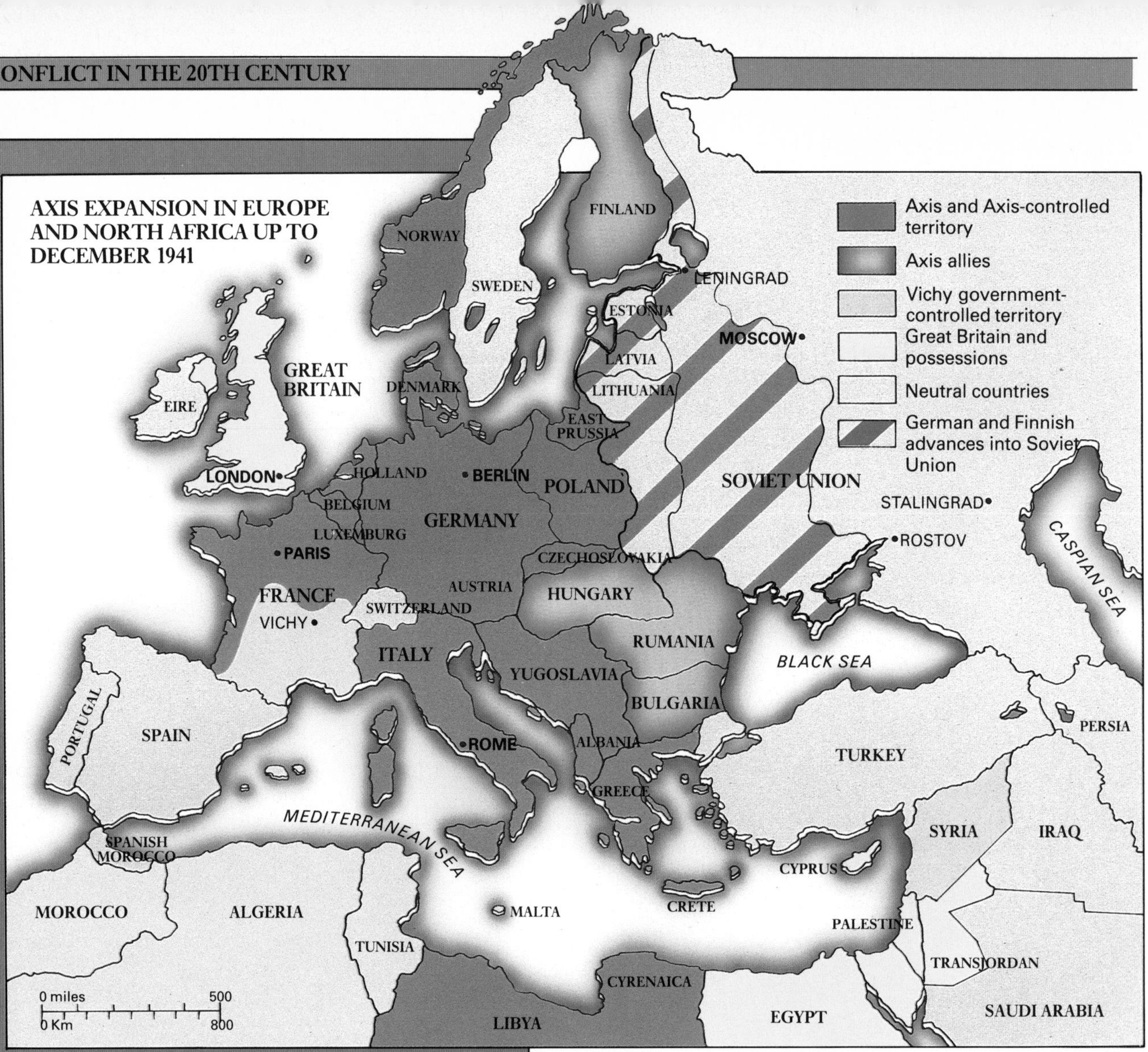

AXIS EXPANSION IN EUROPE AND NORTH AFRICA UP TO DECEMBER 1941

Map legend:
- Axis and Axis-controlled territory
- Axis allies
- Vichy government-controlled territory
- Great Britain and possessions
- Neutral countries
- German and Finnish advances into Soviet Union

Map labels: NORWAY, FINLAND, LENINGRAD, SWEDEN, ESTONIA, MOSCOW, LATVIA, LITHUANIA, EAST PRUSSIA, SOVIET UNION, STALINGRAD, ROSTOV, CASPIAN SEA, GREAT BRITAIN, EIRE, DENMARK, HOLLAND, BERLIN, POLAND, LONDON, BELGIUM, GERMANY, LUXEMBURG, PARIS, CZECHOSLOVAKIA, AUSTRIA, HUNGARY, FRANCE, VICHY, SWITZERLAND, RUMANIA, ITALY, YUGOSLAVIA, BLACK SEA, BULGARIA, PORTUGAL, SPAIN, ROME, ALBANIA, TURKEY, PERSIA, GREECE, SYRIA, IRAQ, MEDITERRANEAN SEA, CYPRUS, SPANISH MOROCCO, MALTA, CRETE, PALESTINE, MOROCCO, ALGERIA, TUNISIA, CYRENAICA, LIBYA, EGYPT, TRANSJORDAN, SAUDI ARABIA

0 miles 500
0 Km 800

CHAPTER 1
A EUROPEAN CONFLICT 1939-1941

Early on September 1, 1939, the Germans invaded Poland. Britain and France declared war on Germany, but could not give any real support to their ally. The Soviet Union took advantage of this to seize the eastern part of Poland. In spring 1940 Hitler turned westward, overrunning Norway and Denmark and then France and the Low Countries. Britain, together with her empire, fought on alone winning the aerial Battle of Britain in the summer of 1940. Then, in June 1941, Hitler invaded the Soviet Union, and Britain was no longer on her own.

During the night of August 31, 1939, men dressed in Polish Army uniforms attacked a German radio station, customs post and forestry station close to the Polish border. Within a few hours German aircraft were bombing Polish airfields, and German tanks and infantry were thrusting across the border. The Second World War had begun.

Because Britain and France had publicly expressed their determination to stand by Poland if Germany should attack her, the German leader Adolf Hitler realized that he would not be able to annex her as easily as he had Austria and Czechoslovakia. In the face of fierce competition from Britain and France, Hitler had managed to negotiate a nonaggression pact with the Soviet leader, Joseph Stalin, on August 23, ensuring Soviet cooperation in the invasion of Poland. All that was now required was a pretext to invade. The incidents on the Polish border were staged by Heinrich Himmler's *Schutz Staffeln* (SS), using concentration camp prisoners to play the part of the Polish soldiers.

The British and French response

In spite of great gallantry, the Polish forces proved no match for the Germans. Using tanks and dive-bombers, the Germans were fighting a new mobile form of warfare, *Blitzkrieg* or "lightning war." This was designed to paralyze the enemy through the sheer speed of the operations. All the Poles could hope for was that Britain and France could relieve the pressure on them by attacking Germany in the West.

The French, at least, hoped that war could still be averted and tried to get the Italian leader, Benito Mussolini, to convene a conference. In Britain, where the inevitability of war had been viewed with increasing fatalism during 1939, Parliament forced Prime Minister Neville Chamberlain to deliver an ultimatum to Hitler that he must withdraw his forces from Poland. Since there was no reply, Britain declared war at 11am on September 3 and France quickly followed suit. For the time being, Italy did not become involved. The United States, still adopting the policy of isolation which had kept her out of European affairs for the past twenty years, declared her neutrality on September 5.

Polish hopes of positive action by the Western Allies were quickly dashed. The French tentatively sent some patrols into the Saarland, but that was all. They had no intention of sacrificing the security of the Maginot Line by advancing into Germany. Meanwhile, the British, as they had done in 1914, sent a small expeditionary force across to France, placing it under the overall command of their ally.

At sea there was to be no mighty clash of battle fleets; Hitler had too much respect for the Royal Navy. Instead, he launched a U-boat (submarine) campaign against British trade, and the first victim was the liner SS *Athenia*, sunk by a U-boat in the belief that she was an armed merchant ship, only hours after Britain had declared war. The British answer was to institute the convoy system in which a group of merchant ships sail together protected by warships. This system had proved very effective during the First World War.

In the air, the prewar belief that a major war in Europe would be marked by immediate bomber attacks on population centers did not materialize. The bomber fleets of both sides were under strict instructions not to attack civilian targets. French fears that attacks on military targets might cause civilian casualties and lead to German reprisals, restricted Allied air operations to leaflet raids and attacks on German seaports.

Polish light tanks stand little chance against the German Blitzkrieg.

The fall of Poland

By September 16, the Germans had surrounded Warsaw, but the city refused to surrender. They now treated it as a military target, subjecting it to savage air and land bombardment. Next day, the Soviets attacked Poland from the East. Ten days later, Warsaw fell and by October 6 all resistance had been crushed.

The USSR and Germany partitioned Poland roughly along the line of the Bug River, with Soviet Russia also occupying the independent Baltic states of Estonia, Latvia and Lithuania. Some Poles managed to escape to the West, and a government in exile was set up by General Wladyslaw Sikorski in Paris. Hitler declared that Britain and France should accept the new situation in Eastern Europe and make peace. Both scornfully rejected this.

The Phony War

On October 9, Hitler issued orders to his generals to carry out an attack in the West as soon as possible. He envisaged a repeat of 1914, with a massive wheel – a sweeping attack through Belgium, but including Holland.

However, his generals wanted time to digest the lessons of Poland and reorganize their forces for what they saw as a much harder task than Poland had been. There was therefore a lull, which came to be known as the Phony War or *Sitzkrieg*. The British and French took the opportunity to continue preparations for the onslaught. Their plan involved moving into Belgium to forestall the German wheel before it entered France. The snag was that Belgium was neutral and refused to allow Allied soldiers into the country.

Elsewhere, there was more activity. German U-boats scored successes against the Royal Navy, sinking an aircraft carrier and the battleship *Royal Oak*, the latter in the fleet anchorage at Scapa Flow in the Shetlands. Merchant ship sinkings rose dramatically, and the only bright spot was in December when three British ships cornered the German pocket battleship *Graf Spee* in the Plate River in South America, forcing her crew to scuttle her. In the air, the picture was equally bleak for the Allies. Bad weather hampered operations, and British bomber attacks by day on German naval bases met with heavy losses.

Adolf Hitler, surrounded by his generals, watches the attack on Warsaw on September 22, 1939.

The Russo-Finnish War

At the end of November 1939, Allied attention turned to Scandinavia. The Soviets had been demanding 30-year leases on Finnish territory, which would give the Soviet Union vital ports in northern waters. When the Finns refused to agree to this, the Soviets invaded.

To the surprise of the West, the Finns stubbornly resisted, and revealed grave shortcomings in the Soviet military machine, resulting largely from the effects of Stalin's purges of his top commanders a few years earlier. However, the French and British failed to give any material support to the embattled Finns because of the refusal of neutral Norway and Sweden to allow the passage of troops and supplies across their territory. Eventually Soviet might triumphed and the Finns were forced in March 1940 to accept their enemy's terms.

The Germans invade Norway

By this time the Allies had become alarmed at the prospect of the Germans seizing Norway's valuable iron ore deposits and planned to mine the Norwegian coast. The Germans got wind of this and struck in early April, overrunning Denmark in one day and then landing troops from air and sea in Norway. The French and British quickly sent troops to Norway, but they were too ill-equipped and badly organized to do more than merely delay the inevitable. Nevertheless it was not until early June that the last Allied troops were finally evacuated.

Blitzkrieg 1940

On May 10, 1940, the long-awaited German offensive in the West finally opened. During the winter the Germans had refined their plans. Instead of the classic wheel, they decided to concentrate their main effort on the Allied center, just to the north of the end of the Maginot Line, by the French frontier with Luxemburg. This was the hilly and heavily wooded Ardennes region, which the Allies believed was unsuitable for major armored operations.

Preceded by air attacks on Allied airfields and parachute operations, the German Panzer (armored) columns dashed through Luxemburg, eastern Belgium and Holland. The French and British troops in the North moved as planned to take up positions on the Dyle River in Belgium, but this did not prevent the Germans from overrunning Holland in a few days.

Worse, the Allied center began to give way as German armored columns, supported by Junkers Ju 87

The symbol of Blitzkrieg: a Ju 87B Stuka dive bomber.

Stuka dive bombers, broke out of the Ardennes and across the Meuse River. This forced the Allies to pull back in Belgium, and their situation was further aggravated when the Germans in the center now raced across northern France to the Channel, aiming to split the Allied armies and cut off the British.

After just over two weeks' fighting, it became clear to the British commander, Lord John Gort, that his army faced annihilation. Evacuation was the only answer. Accordingly, on May 27, a massive operation was launched by the Royal Navy to bring the troops back across the Channel. Next day, the Belgians surrendered and the British, with French troops, were largely confined to a small area around the port of Dunkirk. During the next week, in what has been called the Miracle of Dunkirk, over 300,000 British, French and Belgian troops were taken off the beaches, although they had to leave almost all their equipment.

The French defeat

Left to fight on their own, the French became increasingly disorganized. The final blow came on June 10, when Italy declared war and invaded the French Riviera. On June 17, the French asked for an armistice, which was signed on June 22 in the very same railway coach at Compiègne that had been used to sign the armistice of November 1918. It was not German superiority in numbers of men and weapons which caused the French defeat. The French had neglected their defenses after the First World War and also did not have the will to fight another costly war.

Hitler was now master of northern Europe. Nazi rulers were installed in all the occupied countries, with only the southern half of France being allowed a very limited form of self-government. Here, the aged French hero of the First World War, Marshal Philippe Pétain, was appointed prime minister. This part of the country became known as Vichy France, after the town in which Pétain's government took up residence.

Some Frenchmen, determined to carry on the fight, joined the Free French banner of General Charles de Gaulle in London, while others set up resistance movements inside France. Jews soon began to fear for their safety, as the Nazis extended the campaign for their extermination. Most people, however, were content to try and live as best they could under the Nazis. It was the same for all the occupied countries.

Britain seeks help

Britain now stood alone, bracing herself for the invasion which seemed certain to happen. Inspired by the bulldog tenacity of Winston Churchill, who had become prime minister on the day that France was invaded, the people set to with a will. To obtain the weapons needed to continue the struggle, Churchill turned to the United States for help.

Although the majority of Americans were not prepared to take part in what they saw as a European conflict, there was much sympathy for Britain. In September 1940, the United States gave Britain fifty destroyers in exchange for the lease of British naval bases in the Caribbean. In March 1941, under a scheme called Lend-Lease, the United States began supplying war materials to Britain and other allies.

Another immediate concern was the French fleet, which had escaped the surrender and sailed to French North Africa, which had declared for Vichy. If the fleet should fall into German hands it would be disastrous for Britain's fortunes at sea, but the French admirals

St Paul's Cathedral survives the London Blitz, May 1941.

refused to surrender their ships to Britain. In July, the Royal Navy bombarded them at Mers-el-Kebir, causing much loss of life among the French sailors. This set Vichy France firmly against Britain, a feeling intensified by the failure of a British and Free French amphibious operation against Dakar in French West Africa in September.

The Battle of Britain

Hitler issued his orders for Operation Sea Lion, the invasion of Britain, on July 16. For his troops to be able to get across the Channel and land, it was essential to have command of the air. The Germans had to destroy the Royal Air Force. For the next two months a desperate battle was waged in the skies above Britain as the RAF's fighters, mainly Hawker Hurricanes and Supermarine Spitfires, fought to turn back the waves of German bombers and fighters. By mid-September, the German air force or *Luftwaffe* had had enough and the threat of invasion receded. Speaking of the RAF pilots who fought in the Battle of Britain, Churchill said: "Never has so much been owed by so many to so few."

Hitler now decided to bomb the British people into submission and throughout the winter of 1940-41 his bombers pounded British cities by night in what the people called the Blitz. In retaliation RAF Bomber Command tried to do the same to German cities.

London's underground stations were used as air raid shelters.

Meanwhile at sea the situation remained grave, especially since the U-boats had the advantage of operating from the French Atlantic ports. Such was their success against merchant shipping that the German U-boat crews called the period of July-October 1940 their first "happy time."

Italian intervention in North Africa

During the latter part of 1940, British attention turned to the Mediterranean. Italy's entry into the war created a threat not just to naval domination of the area, but also to Egypt and East Africa from the large Italian garrisons in Libya and Ethiopia. Indeed, in mid-September, the Italians advanced some 95 km (60 miles) into Egypt before halting and setting up fortified camps, while troops from Ethiopia quickly overran British Somaliland and probed cautiously into Kenya and the Sudan. General Archibald Wavell, commanding the British and Commonwealth troops in the Middle East, was undeterred, however, by the overwhelming numbers of enemy troops.

In early December his Western Desert Force (later called the Eighth Army) launched a major raid against the Italians in Egypt and sent them reeling back into Libya. By early February 1941, Wavell's forces had captured the whole of Cyrenaica, but German troops under General Erwin Rommel were now sent in.

The Royal Navy had hoped to draw the Italian fleet into battle, but without success. Nevertheless, there was a very successful operation on shipping in Taranto on November 11, 1940, in which carrier-based aircraft sank one and crippled two of Italy's six battleships.

Italy invades Greece

Mussolini was having problems elsewhere. The Germans had occupied the Rumanian oilfields at the end of October 1940. Mussolini was angered by this, because he believed they lay in the Italian sphere of influence. To restore Italian prestige, he decided to attack Greece. His troops crossed the border from Albania on October 28, but after initial progress the Greeks turned on the invaders and drove them back into Albania.

Hitler now realized that his ally needed material help and launched another *Blitzkrieg* offensive in early April 1941, quickly overrunning Yugoslavia and then Greece. The Royal Navy was able to evacuate a number of the British, Australian and New Zealand troops sent to assist the Greeks, and many were taken to the island of Crete. This was Hitler's next target, designed to give the Axis powers mastery of the eastern Mediterranean, and the Germans mounted an audacious airborne operation on May 20. By the end of the month the island was in their hands, with the Royal Navy having to carry out yet another evacuation. In the meantime, Rommel had driven the British back into Egypt, with only the fortress of Tobruk holding out.

It was indeed a gloomy time for the British, but there were glimmers of light. By May 1941, the Italians in East Africa and Ethiopia had been defeated. A pro-Fascist revolt in Iraq was put down, and in June 1941, in response to a threat that Vichy French Syria was about to allow the Germans use of facilities there, Wavell invaded, quickly forcing the surrender of the French forces in Syria. Wavell could now concentrate his attention on Egypt and driving Rommel back. Not until November 1941 did this happen, under Wavell's successor Claude Auchinleck. Tobruk was relieved and Cyrenaica recaptured.

Also crucial to British strategy was the island of Malta. As it was, Axis air superiority denied the eastern Mediterranean to British merchant convoys and they had to use the longer route around South Africa to bring supplies to the Middle East. If Malta fell, the Royal Navy would not be able to operate in the Mediterranean. Hitler and Mussolini realized this and launched a prolonged air offensive against the island in January 1941. For the next 18 months Malta held out.

Operation Barbarossa

The greatest boost to British confidence came, however, on June 22, 1941, when Hitler invaded the Soviet Union. In spite of the 1939 nonaggression pact, Hitler's ultimate aim had always been the destruction of the Soviet Union and all it stood for. With Northern and Western Europe, apart from Britain, now firmly under his rule, the moment had arrived. The British had had intelligence reports and knew of these preparations. They warned Stalin, but, although distrustful of Hitler, he took little notice.

The German invasion, code-named Barbarossa, therefore took the Russians largely by surprise. Worse, they were in the middle of a major reorganization and the fact that their troops were concentrated on the frontier, rather than deployed in depth, played into the hands of the German *Blitzkrieg* tactics.

As part of a trade agreement, the Russians had been exporting grain to Germany, and it was only shortly after the last grain train had crossed the Bug River at Brest-Litovsk that the German guns opened fire. Some fifteen minutes later German troops moved into Russian-occupied Poland. Hitler deployed three million men for Barbarossa, including Finns seeking revenge for their defeat of fifteen months before.

German troops in Russia, summer 1941.

A German PzKpfw III, supported by infantry, Rostov, 1941.

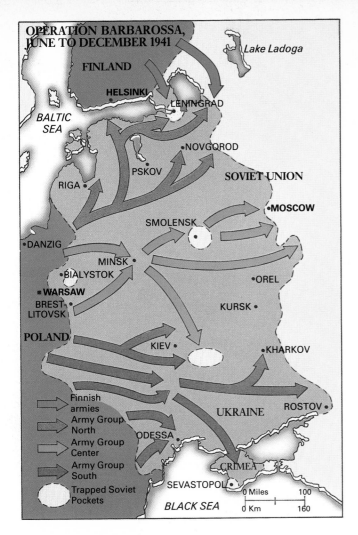

OPERATION BARBAROSSA, JUNE TO DECEMBER 1941

FINLAND

Lake Ladoga

HELSINKI

BALTIC SEA

LENINGRAD

NOVGOROD

PSKOV

RIGA

SOVIET UNION

•MOSCOW

SMOLENSK

•DANZIG

MINSK

•BIALYSTOK

■WARSAW

BREST-LITOVSK

POLAND

KIEV

•OREL

KURSK

•KHARKOV

ROSTOV

UKRAINE

ODESSA

CRIMEA

SEVASTOPOL

BLACK SEA

Finnish armies
Army Group North
Army Group Center
Army Group South
Trapped Soviet Pockets

0 Miles 100
0 Km 160

They were organized into three army groups, North, Center and South. Army Group North was to overrun the Baltic states and link up with the Finns at Leningrad, while Army Group Center had as its ultimate objective Moscow. Army Group South aimed at Kiev and the rich farmlands of the Ukraine.

Within a few weeks, the Germans had scored some spectacular successes. Advancing often as much as 80 km (50 miles) a day, the Panzer columns cut through the Soviet positions and surrounded them, creating enormous pockets of troops who were then forced to surrender to the slower moving bulk of the army, the infantry on their feet. There were enormous hauls of prisoners. The Bialystok pocket produced 290,000, Smolensk 350,000 and Kiev a massive 450,000 men.

As spectacular as these successes were, not everything was going according to plan. Hitler began to interfere increasingly in the day-to-day conduct of operations. Objectives were changed and troops shifted from one army group to another. By September the momentum was beginning to slow down, especially in front of Leningrad, where Army Group North found the lakes and forests hard going. In the center, the Germans were halted by Russian counterattacks.

In October the offensive was renewed once more, but then came the autumn rains, which quickly turned the ground into mud. Snow followed, and the German armies found themselves in the grip of the Russian winter, but without winter clothing. By early December the German advance had ground to a halt, having reached its furthest extent. Leningrad was under siege and the Germans were just 29 km (18 miles) short of Moscow.

Although the Russians had managed to halt the German onslaught, at least temporarily, they were still hard pressed and looked to Britain for support. At the end of September, Britain started sending convoys of weapons around northern Norway to the Soviet port of Murmansk. Otherwise there was little direct support that Britain could give, although the continuing bomber offensive on Germany was beginning to help indirectly by preventing more aircraft being deployed to the Eastern Front, but it was not enough.

One important strategy, which the Russians instituted themselves, was to move much of their industry back behind the Urals, where it was out of range of German aircraft. Also there were a growing number of partisans operating behind the German lines. While many peasants in the Soviet Union had initially welcomed the Germans, believing that they would restore free enterprise, they were quickly disillusioned by the activities of the SS following up the advancing armies. Their systematic brutalities against the civilian population were in line with Hitler's views that the Russians were a subhuman race.

The Atlantic Charter

As 1941 wore on, there were encouraging signs of more active American support for the British cause. At the end of December 1940, US President Franklin D Roosevelt had publicly declared that the United States must make herself "the great arsenal of democracy."

Then, in August 1941 came the historic meeting between Churchill and Roosevelt on board a warship off Newfoundland. Here they signed the Atlantic Charter, which stated that once the Nazi tyranny of Europe had been overthrown all states, both great and small, would be allowed to choose their own form of government and that their integrity would be respected. The Charter was later signed by the Soviet Union, and also by the various governments in exile. Yet the United States was still not at war, even though signing the charter prepared the way. Roosevelt still believed that he could not carry the American people with him.

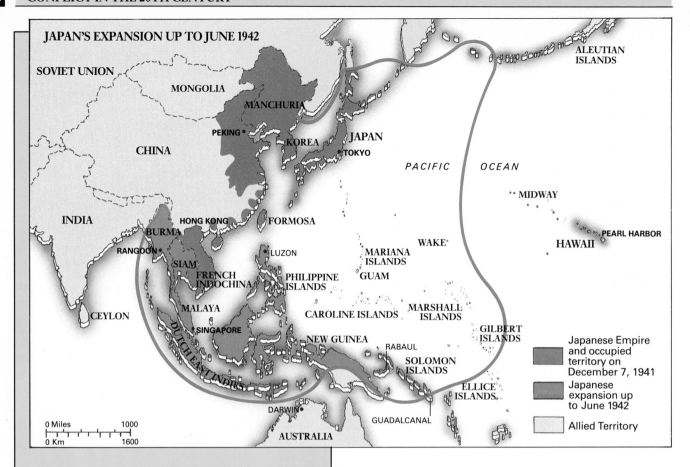

JAPAN'S EXPANSION UP TO JUNE 1942

Japanese Empire and occupied territory on December 7, 1941

Japanese expansion up to June 1942

Allied Territory

CHAPTER 2
GLOBAL WAR 1941-1943

The surprise Japanese attack on the naval base at Pearl Harbor finally brought the United States into the war, but this did not mean an immediate improvement in British or Soviet fortunes. The latter remained under intense German pressure. The British were almost driven back to the gates of Cairo by the Germans, and the Japanese swept all before them in the Pacific and Southeast Asia. Gradually, however, the situation began to change. The Japanese advance was halted; the Germans were stopped and then driven out of Libya and into Tunisia. The Russians trapped a German army in Stalingrad and the final German offensive in Russia in July 1943 petered out. Sicily and then Italy were invaded and the Italians joined the Allies. The Americans began their "island-hopping" in the Pacific.

Throughout the late 1930s Japan had continued to wage war in China against the forces of Chiang Kai-shek, the Chinese leader. In order to achieve her ambition of an empire, however, she looked increasingly toward the wealth-producing colonies of the Western Powers: French Indochina (now Vietnam, Laos and Kampuchea) with its vast rice fields; Burma and Malaya, under British rule, with their tin, oil and rubber; and the Dutch East Indies with their oilfields. It was her plan to create a Greater East Asia Co-prosperity Sphere, taking in a crescent running from the Japanese islands round through the Pacific islands and Dutch East Indies to the Burma-India border.

In order to enlist allies in Europe, Japan signed a Tripartite Pact with Germany and Italy in September 1940, and a neutrality agreement with the Soviet Union in April 1941. On July 24, 1941, Japanese troops peacefully occupied a defenseless French Indochina. At the same time, she had been mounting a diplomatic campaign to persuade the United States that she should have a free hand in Southeast Asia, but Roosevelt would not allow this. It was clear that the Philippines, under the rule of the United States since 1898, came under the Japanese scheme.

There was also American sympathy for Chiang Kai-shek, which was now being expressed in the form of arms and equipment being supplied to him. Two days after the Japanese takeover of French Indochina, the United States and Britain froze Japanese assets, thereby ending the export of all raw materials to Japan. Relations between Japan and the Western Powers worsened, and this was aggravated when a very militaristic Japanese government, led by General Hideki Tojo, came to power in October 1941.

American codebreakers became aware, as November 1941 wore on, that the Japanese were preparing to go to war if the United States did not agree to their demands. Realizing that the Japanese could not succeed as long as they faced the US Pacific Fleet, based at Pearl Harbor in Hawaii, Tojo planned to destroy it in its port. Accordingly, his aircraft carriers set sail. The US codebreakers were able to deduce, from Japanese signals to their ships, that an invasion of Southeast Asia was about to take place. However, the Japanese carriers maintained radio silence, so there was no indication of their destination.

Japan attacks Pearl Harbor

At 7 A.M. on Sunday, December 7, 1941, US radars at Pearl Harbor picked up echoes of a large number of aircraft approaching from the North. They were thought to be American planes so the alarm was not sounded. Some 30 minutes later, the first Japanese aircraft were overhead. In all, 350 Japanese aircraft attacked over the course of two hours, destroying the same number of US aircraft, mostly on the ground, sinking or damaging 18 warships and killing some 3,700 sailors, Marines and civilians.

This was not, however, the only Japanese operation that day. Simultaneously, Midway, an island northwest of Pearl Harbor, was bombarded by warships. Wake Island, 1,600 km (1,000 miles) southwest of Midway, was attacked from the air, as was Guam, 2,400 km (1,500 miles) west of Wake. Japanese troops crossed the border with China to invade the British colony of Hong Kong. Singapore and Malayan airfields were subjected to air attack, as was the US air base at Clark Field in the Philippines. Japanese troops also landed in southern Thailand (Siam) and the north of Malaya.

US destroyers lie in ruins following Japanese raid on Pearl Harbor.

The United States enters the war

In the United States these attacks were greeted with outrage and dismay that the Japanese could have achieved such total surprise. On the West Coast panic set in, since people believed that they would be the next Japanese target. The US government responded by ordering the wholesale imprisonment of Japanese Americans. The British had also rounded up people of German and Italian origin in 1939.

On the political front, the United States and Britain formally declared war on Japan, but the Soviet Union did not and indeed maintained her neutrality almost to the end of the war. On December 11, Germany and Italy declared war on the United States. This was a mistake on Hitler's part, since, although it was probably inevitable that the United States would be eventually drawn into the European war, it meant that she had to give active support to Britain from the outset, rather than devoting her attention solely to Japan.

As it was, faced with a two-ocean war, the United States had to decide where her priorities lay. To do this, Roosevelt and Churchill, with their military staffs, met for a conference in Washington (code named Arcadia) just two weeks after the attack on Pearl Harbor. In spite of opposition from the US Navy, they decided that priority must lie with the defeat of Germany, the policy of "Germany first." The United States would send troops and equipment to Britain with a view to preparing an invasion of Europe. At the same time, they re-endorsed the Atlantic Charter, which was to become the foundation stone of the United Nations.

The Fall of Singapore

In the meantime, the situation went from bad to worse in the Far East and Southeast Asia. Guam and then Wake quickly fell to the Japanese. On Christmas Day 1941, the British garrison on Hong Kong was forced to surrender, and on December 10 the Japanese landed on Luzon in the Philippines. In Malaya, too, they were sweeping all before them. It was here that prewar misconceptions, on the British side, led to defeat.

Singapore, at the southern end of the Malayan peninsula, had always been regarded as Britain's major naval base in the Far East, and it was originally believed that, should war break out, it could be defended by the Royal Navy. In 1939, however, there were not the ships to spare, so the RAF took over the major responsibility, believing that air power would be enough to turn back any invasion of Singapore and Malaya. Coupled to this was the belief that the Japanese were incapable of understanding modern warfare and had inferior weapons. Malaya proved how wrong all this was.

On December 10 Japanese aircraft sank the Royal Navy's two capital ships which had been sent to the area, the *Prince of Wales* and *Repulse*. On land, even though for the most part equipped with only bicycles as transport, Japanese troops easily maneuvered the British and Commonwealth troops out of their positions for the simple reason that they used the jungle, which the defenders did not. On February 15, 1942 Singapore surrendered, to the shock of the British people, who had believed it would never fall.

Within a few days the Dutch East Indies were also in Japanese hands. The Japanese were also driving the British out of Burma. Rangoon had fallen on March 7; by the end of April, with the capture of Lashio and Mandalay, Burma was entirely in Japanese hands and overland communications with Chiang Kai-shek and his forces in China were cut off.

On February 19, the war was brought to the Australian people when Japanese aircraft bombed Darwin; in early April a Japanese naval task force bombed Ceylon (now Sri Lanka) and sank a number of merchant ships in the Bay of Bengal.

A British soldier surrenders, Malaya, 1941.

A Japanese artillery unit on the Bataan Peninsula in the Philippines, 1942.

The Japanese invasion of the Philippines

This left the Philippines, where by early January 1942 the American and Filipino troops had been forced back to the Bataan Peninsula on the west side of Manila Bay. In February, Roosevelt ordered the US commander in the Philippines, General Douglas MacArthur, to Australia to take command of the remaining Allied troops.

He was succeeded by General Jonathan Wainwright, who was forced on April 9 to surrender Bataan because of starvation. The treatment of the survivors, especially during the Bataan Death March, on their way to prison camp was inhuman. Indeed, Allied prisoners of war (POWs) quickly discovered that their Japanese captors viewed surrender in battle as dishonorable, so the POWs lost all status as soldiers. Some managed to escape to the island of Corregidor, which fell on May 6.

At Pearl Harbor, the Japanese had missed the US aircraft carriers which had been out at sea. In early May, two of these carriers were able to foil a Japanese attempt to land on the island of New Guinea at Port Moresby. US carrier aircraft badly damaged one Japanese carrier, but the US carrier *Lexington* was also damaged, and later sank. The Battle of the Coral Sea, as it was called, was significant in that for the first time the Japanese had been checked.

The war at sea

If the war for the Allies was going badly in the Far East, it was no better elsewhere. German U-boats had discovered rich pickings off the eastern seaboard of the United States. Unlike the British, the Americans were slow to introduce convoys especially for maritime shipping between the Gulf of Mexico and Canada, and their antisubmarine naval forces were sparse. The U-boats took full advantage of this in their second "happy time" and during the first six months of 1942 no less than 500 ships were sunk in the area. For a while even the advantages of the convoy system seemed minor.

The convoys from Britain to the Soviet Union also suffered at the hands of German aircraft based in Norway. One convoy, known as PQ17, which sailed for Archangel at the end of June 1942, lost no less than twenty-four of its thirty-five merchant ships.

A further setback had occurred in February, when, in order to escape bombing by the RAF, three of Hitler's most important warships, *Scharnhorst*, *Gneisenau* and *Prinz Eugen*, managed to slip out of the French port of Brest and sail in broad daylight up the English Channel and home to Germany. This was called the Channel Dash and was seen as a great insult to British naval power.

The Eastern Front

On the Eastern Front the Russians were under renewed pressure with the coming of spring. Hitler decreed that the Caucasus, with its extensive oilfields, was to be the major objective, while in the center and North the Germans were to maintain a policy of active defense. However Leningrad, whose inhabitants had stubbornly resisted the Germans during the winter of 1941-42, was to be taken.

The Russians managed to strike first when, on May 12, Marshal Semyon Timoshenko launched an offensive to recapture Kharkov. Initially it went well and the Germans were driven back, but then he was counterattacked in both flanks. Stalin refused Timoshenko permission to withdraw and the bulk of his forces were surrounded; over 250,000 prisoners fell into German hands.

The first phase of the German offensive had begun in early May with attacks aimed at seizing the rest of the Crimea, part of which had been overrun in September 1941. From the Crimea the Germans could cross over onto the Kuban Peninsula and support the main attack on the Caucasus, coming from the north. The Crimea was quickly overrun, except for the port of Sevastopol, which held out until the beginning of July. By this time, the main attack had been launched. The German Panzer columns first advanced east to the Don River and then wheeled south, but they were unable to capture the large numbers of prisoners of 1941 because the Russians withdrew.

The rapid rate of advance also caused supply problems, and the tanks were often forced to halt because of lack of fuel. The farther south the Germans went, the more serious the supply problem became. Their forces were also being dispersed because Hitler was becoming obsessed by the city of Stalingrad. The original plan had been to capture Stalingrad, an important communications center, in order to secure the left flank of the offensive. The Russians were not prepared to surrender the city, and Hitler drew off more and more troops from the main attack. The closer they got to Stalingrad, the more intense the resistance grew.

German troops follow a Panzer PzKpfw IV tank during the advance into the Caucasus, summer 1942.

Soviet troops, led by a Commissar, surrender.

Eventually, by mid-September, the main offensive had petered out in the foothills of the Caucasus Mountains. The Russians were still under tremendous pressure. Admittedly, their factories beyond the Urals had stepped up production, especially of tanks and aircraft, but the need for supplies of equipment from the Western Allies remained. While the British Arctic convoys continued, the Americans opened up another supply route through Persia (now Iran).

Allied strategy

While these supplies helped the Russians, they did not relieve the German pressure directly. What Stalin really wanted was for the Western Allies to invade Europe as soon as possible, and as 1942 wore on he increased his calls for the "Second Front" to be opened. This provoked arguments between the American and British planners. While both sides agreed that victory in Europe could not be achieved without an invasion of the Continent, the British wanted to clear the Axis forces from North Africa first, but the Americans regarded this theater as merely a "sideshow" and agitated for the invasion of France by the end of 1942.

The British thought this was overly optimistic, arguing that if the troops failed to get ashore and establish themselves it would be a grave setback and might prolong the war for years. Furthermore, a very large number of landing craft would be needed and it became clear that these were going to take longer to produce than was originally forecast. At the end of July 1942, however, President Roosevelt backed up the British, when he announced his support for an Anglo-American invasion of French North Africa. This operation would take the Axis forces in Libya in the rear, and it was agreed that it should be mounted by the end of October 1942. Appointed in overall command was General Dwight D Eisenhower.

On August 19, 1942, a Canadian division mounted a major cross-Channel raid on the French port of Dieppe. It was a disaster, with few troops managing to get off the beach and many being killed or captured. Much controversy has surrounded this operation ever since, but what it did demonstrate was that there was a long way to go before an invasion attempt could be mounted with any confidence and that it should not be directed against a port. Nevertheless, Stalin was very displeased when Churchill told him in person in Moscow in August 1942 that there would be no second front that year.

The Battle of El Alamein

In Libya, at the end of January 1942, Rommel attacked the British Eighth Army once more and drove it out of western Cyrenaica. There was now a pause, while both sides prepared for a fresh offensive.

As it happened, it was Rommel who struck first at the end of May, driving the British from their poorly laid-out Gazala Line. After some fierce tank battles, the British were forced to evacuate Libya again and Tobruk, whose defenses had been allowed to deteriorate, fell quickly. By the end of June, the Eighth Army was back on the El Alamein Line, the last defendable position before Cairo – and Rommel was stopped.

At the end of August Rommel launched another offensive but was quickly repulsed by the new commander of the Eighth Army, General Bernard Montgomery. During the next two months Montgomery built up a massive superiority in men and weapons and then struck the Axis defenses at El Alamein on the night of October 23. After a week's fierce fighting, Rommel had had enough and withdrew from Egypt, this time forever, and a few days later came the Allied invasion of French North Africa, Operation Torch.

Erwin Rommel: the "Desert Fox."

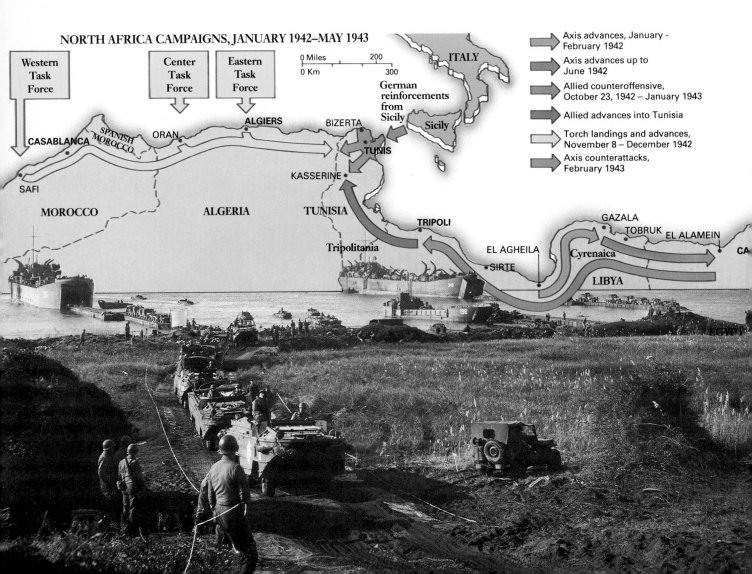

NORTH AFRICA CAMPAIGNS, JANUARY 1942–MAY 1943

Western Task Force

Center Task Force

Eastern Task Force

0 Miles 200
0 Km 300

ITALY

German reinforcements from Sicily

Sicily

CASABLANCA
SPANISH MOROCCO
ORAN
ALGIERS
BIZERTA
TUNIS
SAFI
KASSERINE

MOROCCO
ALGERIA
TUNISIA
TRIPOLI
GAZALA
TOBRUK
EL ALAMEIN

Tripolitania
EL AGHEILA
Cyrenaica
CA

SIRTE
LIBYA

EGYPT

Axis advances, January - February 1942

Axis advances up to June 1942

Allied counteroffensive, October 23, 1942 – January 1943

Allied advances into Tunisia

Torch landings and advances, November 8 – December 1942

Axis counterattacks, February 1943

The Torch landings

Torch marked the US Army's debut in the war in Europe and North Africa. The plan was for three landings to be made, around Casablanca in Morocco and Oran and Algiers in Algeria. The first two landings would be entirely American affairs, while that at Algiers would also involve British forces. The troops taking part in the Casablanca landings were to come direct from the United States, while the others would come from the Clyde River in Scotland.

Crucial to the success of the landings was how the French would react. The United States had not broken off diplomatic relations with Vichy France and was able to establish that the French forces in North Africa would put up only a token resistance and then surrender. To ensure that this would happen, the British troops taking part wore US helmets. The landings took place in the early hours of November 8. In spite of some resistance and casualties to both sides, the landings went relatively smoothly, and it was two days before the French sought an armistice. The Germans retaliated by occupying Vichy France on November 11.

The next step for the Allies was to advance into Tunisia, and a small Anglo-American task force set out from Algiers in order to seize Tunis and Bizerte some 800 km (500 miles) away. The Germans quickly responded to the threat and started to fly in troops from Sicily and Italy, eventually outnumbering their opponents by eight to one. The result was a series of engagements as the opposing forces ran into one another, but the Axis forces had two distinct advantages.

The road and rail communications running into Tunisia from Algiers were sparse, which meant that it was very difficult to keep Allied troops in Tunisia supplied. Also, Allied aircraft were operating off grass fields, which quickly turned to mud in the autumn rains, while the Axis had concrete runways and were soon able to gain air superiority.

Nevertheless, Allied troops did get to within 24 km (15 miles) of Tunis before being driven back. By the end of the year, however, there was an apparent stalemate. Meanwhile Montgomery pursued Rommel through Cyrenaica and Tripolitania, but try as he might, he was never able to trap Rommel and destroy his forces completely.

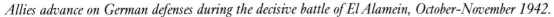

Allies advance on German defenses during the decisive battle of El Alamein, October-November 1942.

The Battle of Midway

The latter half of 1942 saw the tide gradually begin to turn in favor of the Allies in the Pacific. Toward the end of May, the US codebreakers established that the next Japanese objective was the island of Midway, lying 1,760 km (1,100 miles) northwest of Pearl Harbor. Admiral Chester Nimitz sent three carriers to intercept the Japanese fleet, which had four carriers.

While Admiral Chuichi Nagumo's aircraft were engaged in attacking shore targets on Midway, the US aircraft struck. By the end of the day, June 4, all four Japanese carriers had been destroyed, with the Americans only losing the veteran of the Coral Sea, *Yorktown*. It was a clearcut victory, but it did not deter the Japanese from pressing on with their plans to complete the capture of New Guinea and the Solomon Islands. The Allies decided that the Japanese must be driven out of both areas.

The Solomons and New Guinea Campaigns

On August 7, 1942 the first of many amphibious landings in the Pacific took place, when US Marines landed on Guadalcanal, one of the southernmost of the Solomon Islands. The Japanese Navy quickly retaliated by driving the supporting shipping away from Guadalcanal, thus leaving the Marines with no air support until they had, by August 17, built their own airfield on the island. Nevertheless the Japanese, landing reinforcements from their base in Rabaul, made repeated efforts to repulse the Americans. These attacks continued until the end of the year, when the Americans began to drive them back. By now, the Americans had learned that the Japanese would always die rather than surrender and the fighting was brutal.

In the Papua Peninsula of New Guinea, the Japanese managed to establish themselves at Buna, opposite Port Moresby. They advanced over the Owen Stanley Range toward Port Moresby. By September, the Australians and Americans had stopped their advance and slowly began to push the Japanese back to Buna, which they besieged from November.

Burma

In Burma, the picture was bleak. With land communications with Chiang Kai-shek now cut, the United States could only maintain a supply of weapons and equipment to him by air, from Assam over the eastern Himalayas. Known by the pilots as the Hump, it was the toughest air route in the world, but the supplies were flown in.

General "Vinegar Joe" Stilwell was appointed to advise Chiang Kai-shek. He and General Archibald Wavell, now the British commander-in-chief in India, agreed that northern and central Burma must be recaptured as soon as possible so that land communications with China could be restored.

Trying to save the Yorktown *at Midway, June 4, 1942.*

It would take many months to reequip and train the Chinese, British and Indian forces to do this. This was aggravated by widespread internal unrest in India. Mahatma Gandhi had started a "quit India" campaign against British rule. This meant that many troops had to be diverted to internal security duties.

In the meantime Churchill, impatient for action as always, wanted Wavell to advance into the Arakan in western Burma and recapture Rangoon. Wavell saw this as too ambitious, especially since he was short of landing craft as well as trained and equipped troops. Most of the landing craft in the theater were tied up in the operations on Madagascar, which the British had invaded in May 1942 in order to prevent the Japanese using it as a base, and Vichy French resistance there did not end until early November 1942.

Wavell, therefore, decided to invade the Arakan with a single division in order to recapture Akyab (now Sittwe), which the Japanese were using as an aircraft base to dominate the Bay of Bengal. Launched in November, this operation became bogged down by the end of the year, with an inadequate supply system and much sickness from malaria severely denting the morale of the troops.

The Battle of Stalingrad

The Germans on the Eastern Front in autumn 1942 were now facing the prospect of another Russian winter. Although they were better prepared for it than they had been the previous year, they found that the climate was often more bitter than the fighting. They had not yet captured Leningrad and the Soviets continued to deny them Stalingrad.

The German Sixth Army under General Friedrich Paulus, trying to capture Stalingrad, had its flanks protected by Rumanian formations. The Soviets identified them as weak and on November 19, 1942, launched a sudden counterattack on both flanks. Within a few days Paulus was cut off with 220,000 troops. Efforts to supply the surrounded troops by air, followed by an attempt in mid-December to relieve Paulus, both failed, and Hitler refused to allow him to break out of the trap in which he found himself.

As the German relief operation ground to a halt, so the Russians launched fresh attacks, driving the Germans back toward the Donetz River. This threatened the rear of the German armies on the lower Don and in the Caucasus, and at the beginning of January 1943 Hitler was forced to order them to withdraw. The Russian grip around Stalingrad meanwhile tightened.

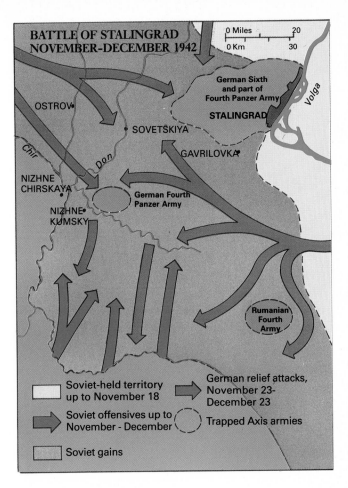

Allied planning for 1943

On January 14, 1943, Roosevelt and Churchill began their third meeting of the war, at Casablanca in Morocco. The main object was to decide what to do after North Africa had been cleared and also to confirm the overall strategy for victory. A number of major decisions were made. For a start, the policy of "Germany first" was reaffirmed.

Roosevelt also demanded and obtained agreement for the unconditional surrender of both Germany and Japan. At the end of the First World War the German armies in the field were not actually defeated. This meant Hitler and his followers could claim that the soldiers had been "stabbed in the back" by the politicians, who agreed to the armistice. In order that this myth could not be repeated, Roosevelt argued that the Allied aim must be to crush German and Japanese military power once and for all. There would be no question of the limited occupation of Germany as in 1918. Both Germany and Japan must be overrun and occupied as a whole.

In hindsight, it is possible that this decision prolonged the war in that the German and Japanese people had everything to lose whether they surrendered or not.

There was nothing to gain by not carrying on fighting, especially if, as their leaders told them, miracle weapons could help turn certain defeat into victory.

As far as the US planners were concerned, the next objective was the invasion of France. Churchill and his military commanders argued, however, that it would be better first to knock out Italy, the weakest member of the enemy alliance. The next target should be Sicily, which was an ideal launching pad for the invasion of the Italian mainland, which Churchill called "the soft underbelly of Europe."

Once again, Roosevelt, perhaps conscious that the British still held the upper hand when it came to forces actually in contact with the enemy, overrode his military advisers and agreed with Churchill. Nevertheless, US troops would continue to be sent to Britain in preparation for the invasion of France, and serious planning for this would begin in April 1943.

Two other important decisions taken were that the transatlantic sea routes must be freed from the danger of the U-boats and that an Anglo-American bombing offensive against Germany be mounted. The Allied leaders recognized the importance of winning the Battle of the Atlantic. Unless the flow of men and, more important, war materials was stepped up, the Allies would not have the resources to carry out their plans. Indeed, Roosevelt had been as good as his word in making the United States "the great arsenal of democracy." The switch of American industry from a peacetime to wartime footing had been a masterpiece of organization. All the Allied forces were relying to an increasing extent on US weapons and equipment.

German defeat in North Africa

In North Africa, on January 23, 1943, Montgomery captured the port of Tripoli, which was vital if his supply line was not to become overstretched. Rommel decided to cross into Tunisia to join the Axis troops, under General Dietloff Jürgen von Arnim, who were already there. Von Arnim made a series of probing attacks on the French, British and American positions in western Tunisia at the end of January. This was a preliminary to a much more serious offensive launched by von Arnim and Rommel in mid-February. On February 14, while von Arnim attacked in the North, Rommel launched his desert veterans against the Americans in the center of the line. They were taken by surprise and the important Kasserine Pass was captured.

The British army commander in Tunisia sent reinforcements to plug the gaps and Rommel's assault

September 9
US Fifth Army

Invading armies and dates
Advances up to August 17
Advances up to September 14
Advances up to September 28
Advances up to December 27

September
British Eigl
Army

**THE INVASION OF ITALY
JULY TO DECEMBER 194:**

0 Miles   100
0 Km   160

July 10
US Seventh Army

July 10
British Eighth Army

petered out. Kasserine had, however, given the Americans a nasty shock and showed that they had much to learn. Eisenhower got rid of the American commander and replaced him with General George S Patton, who could be guaranteed to stiffen the resolve of the troops.

Rommel now turned on Montgomery, was repulsed at Medenine and shortly afterward left North Africa for good. Gradually the Allies pressed the remaining Axis forces back, but not without some bitter fighting. It was only in mid-May that the Italian and German forces finally surrendered, 200,000 prisoners falling into Allied hands.

The invasion of Italy

Planning for the invasion of Sicily had begun in April, while the campaign in Tunisia was still being fought. In essence, Patton's US Seventh Army would clear the West of the island, while Montgomery's Eighth Army tackled the East. The ultimate objective was Messina on the northeast corner, which was only 8 km (5 miles) from the Italian mainland. Hopes that the island would be quickly overrun were soon dashed.

Although the troops got ashore with little difficulty, the mountainous country, the summer heat and the determined German defense meant that it was not until August 17 that Messina was reached and, even then, the defenders managed to escape to the mainland.

Three weeks later, the Allies landed in Italy. Montgomery crossed the Strait of Messina and began to work his way up the "toe" of Italy, while on the same day General Mark Clark's US Fifth Army landed at Salerno, south of Naples.

Following the invasion of Sicily, the Italians sought and were granted an armistice. The feeling had been growing among the Italian people that it was pointless to continue the war in the face of so many reverses. On July 25, Mussolini was overthrown and the king of Italy, Victor Emmanuel III, who up until that time had been a mere figurehead, appointed Marshal Pietro Badoglio as prime minister with orders to make peace with the Allies.

Mussolini was arrested and thrown into prison, although he was later rescued by the Germans in a daring airborne operation. It took time, however, for the negotiations to be concluded with the Allies and the surrender was only announced on September 8. Although taken by surprise, the Germans reacted quickly, rushing troops across the Brenner Pass from Germany. A few weeks later, Italy formally joined the Allies, declaring war on Germany.

The bombing offensive against Germany

The agreement to launch a combined bombing offensive on Germany was controversial. The overall aim was to destroy and disrupt the German military, industrial and economic system and to lower the morale of the German people so that their ability to wage war was "fatally weakened." Specific targets were agreed upon, including attacks on shipyards building U-boats to help in the Battle of the Atlantic, but there was a difference of opinion between the British and American air commanders as to how to carry out Pointblank, as this offensive was to be called. The Americans believed that their heavily armed bombers could attack targets accurately by day without losing too many aircraft to German fighters.

RAF Bomber Command, led by Arthur ("Bomber") Harris, on the other hand, had long given up daylight raids and believed that the key to a successful air offensive lay in the night-time bombing of cities, not so much to kill the people who lived there but to destroy their houses and factories. In the end, the two views complemented one another, in that the RAF attacked by night, while the Americans did so by day, in what was called "round the clock" bombing, but this took time to materialize.

The bombing of the Ruhr

The most spectacular bombing raid of the time was that carried out by the RAF's 617 Squadron on the Ruhr dams on the night of May 16. Two dams were destroyed and a third damaged, but eight of the nineteen aircraft involved were lost. Although its effect on German war industry was not decisive, the raid provided an enormous boost to morale.

The Möhne Dam after the RAF attack on the night of May 16, 1943.

This was part of the first of three major offensives which RAF Bomber Command launched in 1943 against the towns and cities of the Ruhr, Germany's major industrial region. It lasted from the beginning of March until the beginning of July. The US Army Air Force (USAAF) also began to enter the fray, escalating the damage and gradually extending its daylight targets deeper into Germany.

The bombing of Hamburg and Schweinfurt

At the end of July, "Bomber" Harris launched four major night raids on the city of Hamburg, with the USAAF making two daylight raids. The devastation was greater than anything so far experienced in the bombing war and such was the intense heat generated that there was a firestorm accompanied by fierce hot winds, in which 400,000 people died.

Intelligence reports showed that the Germans were building rockets to use in a new attack on Britain and RAF Bomber Command raided the experimental station at Peenemünde on the Baltic coast during August 17-18, 1943. Earlier that day, the USAAF had suffered a severe setback when, in an attack on the ball-bearing factory at Schweinfurt, 60 out of 376 bombers were shot down and many others badly damaged. On October 14 another raid on Schweinfurt produced similar losses and the daylight bombing campaign was halted. The bombers needed fighter protection; it would not be until the following year, however, that the P-51 Mustang would be available.

The Battle of the Atlantic

The spring of 1943 saw another of the aims of the Casablanca Conference achieved, that of winning the war against the U-boats in the Atlantic. In March 1943 there had been a sudden rise in the number of merchant ships lost. Bad weather in April prevented the U-boats from increasing their success, but May saw the climax of the long battle.

Hitler's naval commander, Admiral Karl Doenitz, had more U-boats deployed in the Atlantic than at any other time in the war. Yet, it was now that the Allies managed to coordinate their antisubmarine activities – intelligence, sea and air. In just over 20 days no less than 31 U-boats were sunk and Doenitz ordered his U-boats to withdraw temporarily from the Atlantic. In June 1943, for the first time, the rate of Allied merchant ship building was greater than losses. For the remainder of the war the Allies still had to keep their guard up, but the threat of the U-boat diminished.

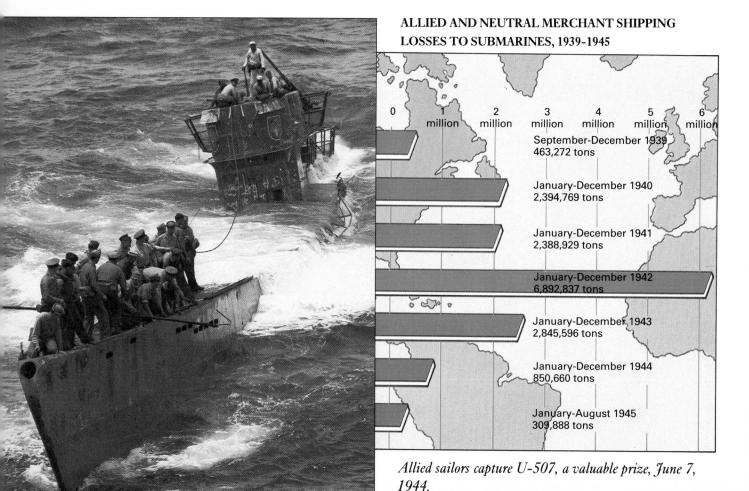

ALLIED AND NEUTRAL MERCHANT SHIPPING LOSSES TO SUBMARINES, 1939-1945

0	1 million	2 million	3 million	4 million	5 million	6 million

September-December 1939
463,272 tons

January-December 1940
2,394,769 tons

January-December 1941
2,388,929 tons

January-December 1942
6,892,837 tons

January-December 1943
2,845,596 tons

January-December 1944
850,660 tons

January-August 1945
309,888 tons

Allied sailors capture U-507, a valuable prize, June 7, 1944.

From Stalingrad to Kursk

On the Eastern Front, the Germans at Stalingrad were remorselessly pounded by the Soviet armies under General Vassili Chuikov. Field Marshal Hermann Goering, the Luftwaffe's commander-in-chief, had assured Hitler that he could keep Paulus supplied from the air, but this proved an idle boast and only a fraction of the supplies needed were received. Apart from the difficulties of landing on icebound airstrips, often under the fire of Soviet guns, the Germans simply did not have enough transport aircraft. One of the reasons for this was the enormous losses they had suffered during the capture of Crete in May 1941.

The Russians then split the German forces in two, and on January 31, 1943, in spite of Hitler's pleas to hold out until the end, Paulus surrendered. Some 70,000 Germans had been killed at Stalingrad and 91,000 surrendered, of whom only 6,000 would eventually return to Germany. It marked the turning point on the Eastern Front, showing that the German Army could be defeated.

By the beginning of March 1943, the Soviets had driven the Germans back to the line of the Donetz River. Attention now switched farther north, to a large salient or bulge which the Soviets had carved out for themselves, with Kursk at its center.

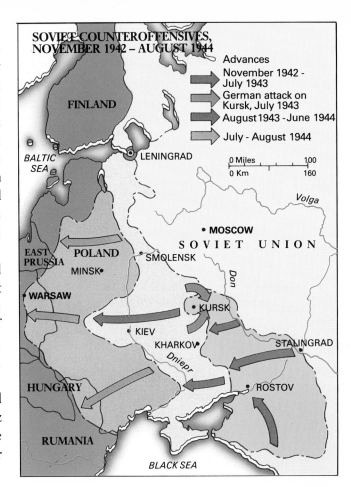

SOVIET COUNTEROFFENSIVES, NOVEMBER 1942 – AUGUST 1944

Advances
November 1942 - July 1943
German attack on Kursk, July 1943
August 1943 - June 1944
July - August 1944

Captured Soviet T-34 tanks, stuck in a marsh near Tolochin.

In mid-April, Hitler gave orders that this salient was to be removed. Army Group Center was to attack from the north and Army Group South from the south. The attacks were originally planned for May 1, as soon as the ground had dried out after the spring thaw, but Hitler then decided that they must be delayed until new heavy tanks could be sent to Russia. In the meantime, the Soviets became well aware of the German plans. They organized their defenses accordingly, constructing a network of antitank strongpoints and minefields.

Consequently, when the Germans finally attacked on July 5, 1943, they found the Russian resistance very much tougher than they expected. Progress was slow. Then, on July 12, the Russians counterattacked to the north of Kursk, and there now took place the largest tank battle of the war. During the Kursk operations some 3,000 tanks were destroyed, but the Soviets, with their factories producing more and more weapons, could afford these losses, while the Germans could not. Hitler halted the offensive, and from then on the German armies in the East would be on the defensive.

Island-hopping in the Pacific

In the Pacific, the tide of fortune had definitely turned in favor of the Allies. The Japanese had evacuated Buna at the end of January 1943, but elsewhere on the Papua Peninsula of New Guinea resistance continued, and it was only at the end of September 1943 that it was finally secured.

The next task facing the Allies in the Pacific, however, was to clear the Japanese from the remaining Solomon Islands. They adopted the technique of "island-hopping," securing one island at a time and bypassing major Japanese bases, such as Rabaul.

On April 18, 1943, the Americans achieved a remarkable coup when they shot down the aircraft carrying the Japanese commander in the Pacific, Admiral Isoroku Yamamoto, the architect of the attack on Pearl Harbor. Gradually the United States progressed up the Solomon Islands, with New Georgia being secured in August, and landings on Bougainville taking place on November 1, 1943.

By this time, the Americans had more than replaced their losses at Pearl Harbor and could afford to turn their attention elsewhere in the Pacific. The operations in New Guinea and the Solomons were denting the Japanese defenses and removing the threat to Australia. However, what was needed was a more direct line of attack on Japan itself. As early as April 1942, in an audacious raid mounted from an aircraft carrier, a squadron of B-25 Mitchells under Lieutenant Colonel James Doolittle had bombed Japan.

US Marines under fire during the assault on Tarawa, in the Gilbert Islands, November 1943.

This was the only attack on the Japanese mainland to be mounted in more than two years. It served as little more than a morale booster for the Allies at a time when the situation in the Pacific was still very grave.

In any event, US planners thought Japan, like Germany, could only be defeated by direct invasion. Consequently another island-hopping campaign was planned with its ultimate objective the Japanese mainland. The first target was the Gilbert Islands. In November 1943, Makin and Tarawa were assaulted, the former falling easily, but the latter only being captured at a high cost in casualties. Some 1,000 US Marines and sailors were killed and 2,000 wounded. The Pacific campaign now had two axes of advance.

Burma

The third Allied pressure point on Japan was in Burma. During the first few months of 1943, the Japanese counterattacked in the Arakan, driving the British and Indian troops there back to Chittagong in India. Much needed to be done before the Allies could launch a campaign to regain Burma.

There was, however, one small success during that summer. This was "long-range penetration" of the Japanese lines. In February 1943 Brigadier Orde Wingate took a brigade of what he called Chindits, after the mythical Burmese beast the *chinthe*, through the Japanese lines and for two months attacked Japanese lines of communication. Although this did not achieve a major impact, the British and Indian soldiers were seen to be as good as the Japanese at jungle fighting. Stilwell's Americans also took up long-range penetration and Merrill's Marauders spent much time operating behind enemy lines in northern Burma during the first half of 1944.

The Tehran Conference

At the end of November 1943 another historic meeting of Allied war leaders took place, this time at Tehran, the capital of Persia (Iran), and involved not just Churchill and Roosevelt, but Stalin as well. The main object was to discuss postwar Europe, and it was Stalin who dominated the proceedings. From the end of 1941 onward, the Soviets had made it clear that Poland was in their sphere of influence and that the border agreed upon with the Germans in 1939 when the country was partitioned was to be Poland's eastern border with the Soviet Union. At Tehran he also proposed that the border with Germany should be moved westward to the Oder River.

The Western Allies did not raise any objections to these proposals. However, the British realized that the Polish government in exile in London would not accept domination by the Soviet Union, any more than by Germany. Matters had been aggravated by the German discovery of a mass grave containing the bodies of some 4,000 Polish officers in the Katyn Forest in Russia. The Germans stated that the Russians had been responsible, but the latter blamed the Germans. The evidence, however, pointed to the Russians, and the Polish government in exile demanded an investigation by the International Red Cross.

At this point Stalin broke off relations with the London Poles. For the sake of Allied unity neither Churchill nor Roosevelt dared to support the Polish case. As for Germany, it was agreed in principle that the country should be partitioned, but the detailed planning of how this was to be done was left to be decided at a later date.

Allied planning

In terms of military strategy, Stalin continued to press for the invasion of France. The campaign in Italy did not impress him. Admittedly, the British and Americans had found the going hard and successive German defense lines meant that progress was slow. By the end of 1943 they were still well to the south of Rome. The fact that they were tying down German forces cut little ice with Stalin.

Stalin eventually managed to secure a promise from Churchill and Roosevelt that the invasion of France would be mounted before the end of May 1944, and that it would comprise landings across the English Channel and in the South of France. Now committed to Overlord and Anvil, as these two operations were code-named, the Western Allies realized that shortage of landing craft would prevent any other amphibious operations being mounted, for example in Burma. One concession that Stalin did make at Tehran was that Russia would join in the war against Japan two months after Germany had been defeated.

Thus, the Allies had agreed on the tasks for 1944. While the Soviets continued to drive the Germans back and out of Russia, the British and Americans would maintain pressure on the Germans in Italy and prepare for what was to be the greatest amphibious operation of all time, across the English Channel. Allied forces would go onto the offensive in Burma, and in the Pacific the two island-hopping offensives would close in on Japan itself.

Allied convoy sweeps through St. Lo, Normandy, July 1944.

CHAPTER 3
VICTORY ROAD
1944-1945

While German forces were kept tied down in Italy, the Allies successfully landed in France and, after bitter fighting in Normandy, quickly liberated the remainder of the country and much of Belgium and southern Holland. Then overstretched supply lines, the coming of winter weather and German recovery slowed them down. In the East the Russians relentlessly drove the Germans out of their country and back into Germany itself. In a last desperate gamble Hitler turned on the Western Allies with a counterattack in December 1944, but it was unsuccessful. After this the end of the war in Europe was only a matter of time. In the Far East the Japanese were gradually driven back across the Pacific toward Japan itself and were also defeated in Burma.

With mobilization and war production reaching new peaks, the Allies were poised for major new offensives. In Europe, resistance movements helped to undermine the Axis from within, at the same time expressing their political allegiances for the postwar settlement.

Throughout 1942 and 1943, resistance movements in the occupied countries had been growing. They received arms and equipment, as well as advisers on the ground, from the American Office of Strategic Services (OSS) and the British Special Operations Executive (SOE). The OSS and SOE agents often had a hard time identifying which resistance groups to back.

In the Balkans the Communists, encouraged by the Soviet Union, used the resistance to seize power at the end of the war. In Yugoslavia, the royalist groups were more concerned to crush Tito's Communist partisans than they were to attack the Germans, and indeed collaborated with the latter. Nevertheless, the part played by the resistance movements in tying down German troops which could have been used elsewhere cannot be underestimated.

The Holocaust

By 1944, time was running out for those Jews held in German concentration camps. Heinrich Himmler believed that the Aryan (German and north European) race was superior to all others and that Jews and Slavs were subhumans, a "harmful influence," and should be eliminated.

In what he called "the final solution," Himmler set about destroying the Jews in Europe. The concentration camps multiplied and when more traditional methods of killing, such as shooting and hanging, did not produce a high enough rate of deaths, he introduced poison-gas chambers into which Jews were herded in droves. Others were sterilized or used as guinea pigs in inhuman medical experiments.

There were constant roundups of Jews and in most occupied countries they were easily recognizable since they were forced to wear a large yellow star on their clothing. In some major cities, notably Warsaw, they were made to live in ghettoes in particular parts of the city. Many, fearing what might happen to them, went into hiding, often sheltered by non-Jewish families, who were fully aware that if they were caught, they too would be sent to a concentration camp.

Non-Jews as well were often parted from their families by being made to go to work in Germany. Indeed, it was largely imported foreign labor that allowed

Parisians dive for cover as beleagured German snipers are flushed out by Resistance fighters, August 25, 1944.

Germany not to mobilize her war economy fully until 1943. In Britain and the Soviet Union, for instance, both men and women who did not join the armed forces were conscripted to work in factories.

Breaking the Gustav Line

Meanwhile in Italy progress was slow. One reason was that before the end of 1943 some troops, mainly seasoned veterans of North Africa, were withdrawn and sent to England to begin preparing for Overlord. The other was the difficulty of the terrain, especially the mountains, which gave the defenders an advantage.

Their next major objective was Rome, but the Allies were held up by the formidable Gustav Line, which the Germans had built 120 km (75 miles) south of the city. In order to get around this, British and American troops landed at Anzio 50 km (30 miles) south of Rome on January 22, 1944. They failed to move quickly inland off the beaches and a swift German response meant that the success of the landings was in the balance for the next five weeks, as the Germans counterattacked. Hopes that Anzio would lead to the German evacuation of the Gustav Line faded and for the next few months the fighting centered on Monte Cassino, with its famous monastery. The fact that Americans, Britons, Canadians, Indians, New Zealanders and Poles are buried here gives some indication of the intensity of the fighting. Not until the latter half of May did the Poles finally capture it, and as forces at Anzio advanced, the Germans withdrew to the north of Rome.

Rome had been declared an "open city." This meant that both sides agreed not to fight in it because of its historic remains and because it was the seat of the Roman Catholic Church. Rome was "liberated" by the Allies at the beginning of June.

The relief of Leningrad

On the Eastern Front, the Soviets had gone over to the offensive immediately after the Battle of Kursk and by the autumn of 1943 had driven the Germans back to the Dniepr River. They now outnumbered the Germans by two to one and their strength and confidence were growing all the time. There was, also, increasing bitterness toward the German invaders as the Russians advanced westward. The country had been entirely desolated by the Germans, and there was much evidence of atrocities against the civilian population. It was therefore understandable that the Russians vowed that when they reached the German borders they would exact revenge in kind.

There was no question that the offensive would pause during the winter months. The Germans must not be given time to regroup, and the Russians were helped in this by the fact that the winter of 1943-44 was unusually mild on the Eastern Front. Their first success came in January when Leningrad was finally relieved. During the 890 days of the siege some 200,000 people had been killed by enemy fire and more than 500,000 had died of cold or starvation.

The Russians now struck blow after blow on the Germans. On January 6, attacking from west of Kiev, they had crossed the prewar border with Poland. The German Army Group North was driven back during the latter half of January and February from south of Leningrad to the Latvian and Estonian borders. In the far South, by mid-April the Soviet armies were poised to enter Hungary and Rumania and were beginning to clear the Crimea. The Germans continued to fight with great skill, but lost men unnecessarily because of Hitler's repeated insistence that they should hold onto positions long after the Russians had bypassed them.

Overlord preparations

The main event in 1944 as far as the Western Allies were concerned was to be Overlord. Once ashore in France, it would only be a matter of time, with the spectacular Soviet advances in the East, before Germany was crushed. Detailed planning for the cross-Channel invasion had begun as early as April 1943 when a special headquarters was set up in England for this purpose. Throughout the next few months, the planners grappled with the problem of where to land.

Intelligence was gathered from many sources on the state of the beaches, tides and German defenses along the entire coastline of northern France. Secret agents, the French Resistance and Commandos were used, along with air photographs and even people's prewar holiday picture postcards. The Germans had been aware from the very beginning that an invasion would be mounted at some time, and had been preparing the coastal defenses for the past three years.

They expected the landings to be in the Pas de Calais since this was the closest point to Britain. For this reason, the Allied planners decided that they must select another spot and chose Normandy. In order to keep this secret from the Germans they evolved elaborate deception plans to make the Germans continue to believe that the Pas de Calais would be used and also to persuade Hitler to keep troops tied down in Norway in case there was an invasion there.

Appointed in overall command of Overlord was General Eisenhower, with General Montgomery to command the actual landings. They both returned to London in January 1944. Training for the British, American and Canadian troops now intensified. At the same time, a number of special devices were developed to help the troops get ashore and keep them supplied. Most notable of these were the artificial Mulberry harbors, which were to be towed across the Channel and anchored offshore so that supply ships could unload. There was also Pluto (Pipeline Under the Ocean), which would be the main means of transporting fuel supplies. Five beaches were selected for the landings: Omaha and Utah for the Americans, and Juno, Gold and Sword farther east for the British and Canadians.

The Allied air forces also had a major part to play. Apart from the direct support for the landings, which meant obliterating the defenses, there were two other key tasks to be carried out. It was crucial that the Allies had air supremacy over the beaches and also that the Germans be prevented from rushing up reserves to drive the invaders back into the sea. In the months leading up to the invasion, the US and RAF strategic bombing offensive against Germany was halted, and the bombers were given the task of attacking aircraft factories and railway marshaling yards.

The D-Day landings

In order to obtain the right weather conditions, especially from the point of view of the tides, Overlord was scheduled for June 5, but bad weather forced a postponement for twenty-four hours. Spearheaded by American and British paratroop operations, and covered by a massive naval bombardment, 70,000 troops stormed ashore on the morning of June 6, 1944, establishing themselves against often stiff resistance. In the next two months, two million Allied troops would be landed in France.

The Germans were taken by surprise, and for a time Hitler was convinced that it was a feint and that the main landings in the Pas de Calais were still to come. He therefore refused to allow Rommel, who was now commanding the anti-invasion forces, to move his tank reserves to Normandy. Nevertheless, the Germans, as was so often the case, quickly recovered from their surprise and for the next two months the Allies found it hard going. In Normandy the winding lanes and little fields enclosed by hedgerows on top of banks very much favored the defender.

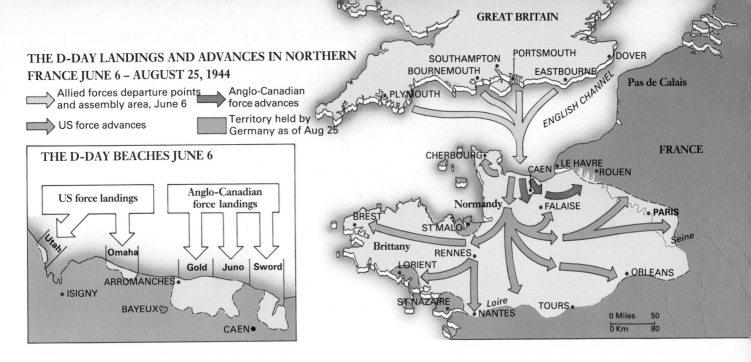

THE D-DAY LANDINGS AND ADVANCES IN NORTHERN FRANCE JUNE 6 – AUGUST 25, 1944

Allied forces departure points and assembly area, June 6

US force advances

Anglo-Canadian force advances

Territory held by Germany as of Aug 25

GREAT BRITAIN

SOUTHAMPTON
PORTSMOUTH
BOURNEMOUTH
EASTBOURNE
DOVER
PLYMOUTH

Pas de Calais

ENGLISH CHANNEL

FRANCE

CHERBOURG
CAEN LE HAVRE
ROUEN
Normandy
FALAISE
PARIS
BREST
ST MALO
Seine
Brittany
RENNES
LORIENT
ORLEANS
ST NAZAIRE
Loire
NANTES
TOURS

0 Miles 50
0 Km 80

THE D-DAY BEACHES JUNE 6

US force landings

Anglo-Canadian force landings

Utah
Omaha
Gold Juno Sword
ARROMANCHES
ISIGNY
BAYEUX
CAEN

The Bomb Plot

On July 20, 1944, while the Western Allies were still battling away in Normandy, a dramatic event occurred in East Prussia. A bomb hidden in a briefcase exploded in a room where Hitler was holding a conference at his field headquarters. There had been a resistance movement in Germany against Hitler for some time, and one previous attempt on his life. This second attempt was the work of a number of senior army officers in conjunction with politicians and priests, who wanted to come to terms with the Allies.

The attempt failed and the conspirators were ruthlessly hunted down. Many were executed. Among the conspirators was Rommel, who three days before had been wounded in France in an air attack. He was later forced to take his own life. The Bomb Plot had little effect on the course of the war except to make Hitler distrust his generals more and more.

British infantry follow a Churchill tank in bocage *country of Normandy, June 1944.*

The liberation of Paris

In July the British and Canadians wore down the German armor in Normandy. Patton's US Third Army then quickly cleared Brittany and moved west and east. The German line was pushed back and soon the Allied tanks were dashing across France in pursuit of a beaten enemy. On August 15, Operation Anvil (now renamed Dragoon), the landings in the south of France, began and General Alexander Patch's US Seventh Army began to move northward to link up with the armies in northern and eastern France.

Ten days later the Germans surrendered Paris to Free French troops, after five days' fighting with the French Resistance. It was apparent that the Communists would try to seize power, but this was forestalled by the arrival of de Gaulle. The British soon reached Belgium and on September 3 Brussels was liberated. It was an exhilarating few weeks for both liberated and liberators alike, but now the Allies faced a problem.

The farther east the Allies moved, the longer their supply lines became. Hopes that they could shorten them were dashed when Hitler ordered that the Channel ports be turned into fortresses. It took time to reduce them and even longer to open them up again to shipping. Consequently, the Allies now began to run short of fuel and were forced to halt, thereby giving the Germans a chance to recover.

There was now a fierce debate on what to do next. Montgomery believed that he could achieve victory by the end of 1944 with a single thrust on Germany.

Eisenhower, however, felt that such a narrow advance could not be adequately supplied and would be extremely vulnerable to attack on the flanks. He was thus determined that the Allies should advance side by side on a broad front, at least as far as the Rhine, even if, because of the supply situation, progress might be very much slower.

Operation Market Garden

Nevertheless, Eisenhower allowed Montgomery to put one of his ideas into action. Ever since D-Day, June 6, 1944, there had been a large airborne army sitting in England waiting to be used. Montgomery had devised a plan for putting pressure on the German flank by seizing crossings over the three major rivers that ran through Holland: the Maas, Waal and Lower Rhine. Eisenhower gave him two US airborne divisions, a British airborne division and a Polish airborne brigade.

On September 17, Operation Market Garden was launched. The Americans successfully seized bridges at Eindhoven and Nijmegen and British ground forces linked up with them, but the farthest objective, at Arnhem, which had been given to the British and Polish paratroopers, proved to be overly ambitious. The link-up forces were constantly held up. After eight days' bitter fighting, the paratroopers were ordered to withdraw from Arnhem, but only 30 per cent arrived back inside the Allied lines. With this failure, the last chance to finish the war in the West before the end of 1944 was gone.

Men of the US 82nd Airborne Division drop near Nijmegen, September 1944.

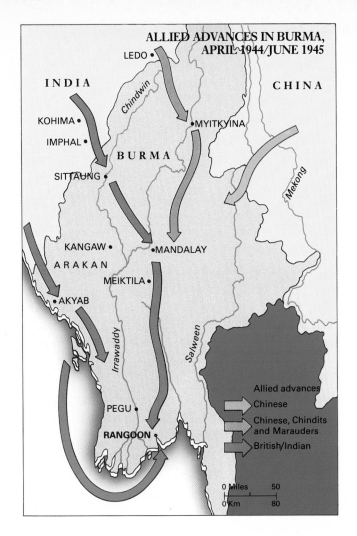

ALLIED ADVANCES IN BURMA,
APRIL 1944/JUNE 1945

INDIA

CHINA

LEDO

KOHIMA

IMPHAL

MYITKYINA

BURMA

SITTAUNG

Chindwin

KANGAW

ARAKAN

MANDALAY

MEIKTILA

AKYAB

Irrawaddy

Salween

Mekong

Allied advances

Chinese

Chinese, Chindits
and Marauders

British/Indian

PEGU

RANGOON

0 Miles   50

0 Km   80

Progress in Burma

The first half of 1944 finally saw an upturn in Burma. Both sides had been preparing to mount attacks, but it was the Japanese who struck first. At the beginning of February, two Indian divisions were advancing steadily into the Arakan, to secure positions for a major attack. They were unexpectedly hit by the Japanese in the flank. On previous occasions the British and Indians had always pulled back, but this time General William Slim, commanding the British Fourteenth Army, ordered his men to stand fast and it worked. After three weeks' bitter fighting the Japanese fell back exhausted.

This also occurred on the central front, which followed the line of the Chindwin River and relied for its supplies on a single road running from the railhead at Dimapur through Kohima and Imphal in India. On March 8, a Japanese army struck at the last two named places. By early April the garrisons of both were surrounded and they became entirely reliant on an airlift system, much of it carried out by the USAAF, for their supplies and reinforcements. After bitter fighting the Japanese were driven back by early July.

In northern Burma, goaded by Stilwell, Chiang Kai-shek had begun to advance from Ledo southward toward Myitkyina. It was slow going not just because of the resolute Japanese defense but also because of Chiang Kai-shek's continual hesitation. Indeed, at one point the Americans threatened to cut off all aid in order to get the Chinese to move. To support the advance, both Merrill's Marauders and Wingate's Chindits were dropped behind the Japanese lines. Eventually Myitkyina was captured on August 3.

A problem now arose in China. The Japanese were carrying out an offensive, directed against both Chiang Kai-shek's forces and those of his Communist rival, Mao Tse-tung. This new offensive was aimed at the Szechuan province in the Southeast, where the Americans had established air bases from which to bomb Japan. The Americans proposed that Stilwell be put in charge of all Chinese forces but Chiang Kai-shek and his advisers had become increasingly disenchanted with Stilwell and used this opportunity to obtain his dismissal. The problem with the threat to the US bombing offensive against Japan was solved, however, by events in the Pacific.

The destruction of Japanese naval aviation

In the Southwest Pacific the Americans and Australians continued to clear New Guinea and the Solomons. By mid-February 1944, New Zealand troops had seized the Green Islands, which put the Allies only 160 km (100 miles) from the main Japanese base at Rabaul. Rather than attempt to capture it, the Allies used air power to neutralize it, and MacArthur moved on to tackle Dutch New Guinea.

It was much the same in the Central Pacific, where Truk, some 3,200 km (2,000 miles) west-northwest of the Gilbert Islands, was the main Japanese base. By mid-February the Marshall Islands were in US hands, again after bitter fighting. This brought them 1,250 km (800 miles) closer to Truk. They now launched air attacks on the base and during two days, February 17-18, 1944, they dropped thirty times as much explosive as the Japanese had on Pearl Harbor and rendered Truk unusable.

Admiral Nimitz, commanding the US forces in the Central Pacific, now turned on the Mariana Islands. US Marines landed on Saipan on June 15, but four days later a Japanese carrier task force attempted to intervene. It was disastrous. In what became known as the Battle of the Philippines Sea, US pilots shot down 244 Japanese aircraft for the loss of just 31 of their own and sank a carrier, while a US submarine accounted for another carrier.

Nevertheless, the Japanese on Saipan fought with their usual determination and lost some 27,000 men. Landings were then made on Guam and Tinian, and by early August the Marianas were in US hands. This meant that the Americans were now within bombing range of Japan, and later in the year they moved their bombing squadrons from China to the Marianas.

US strategy in the Pacific

By now the remainder of New Guinea had been cleared, and MacArthur's and Nimitz's forces were in a commanding position to mount combined operations. As had been the case in Northwest Europe, there was a debate on what to do next. Originally, the American planners had agreed that the next objective should be the Philippines, but as 1944 wore on, alternatives were suggested by the planners.

One was to go straight for Formosa, which would put air power very much closer to Japan. This would mean that heavier bomb loads could be carried and another air supply route could be opened to China. Another was to invade the southernmost island of Japan, Kyushu. Both these ideas, which originated in Washington, envisaged bypassing the Philippines. However, both MacArthur and Nimitz objected that this would be overextending their operations.

It was then agreed that the southern Philippines should be captured first. MacArthur, who had vowed to the Filipinos when he left in early 1942 that he would return, argued that the Americans were duty bound to liberate all the Philippines, including the northernmost and main island of Luzon, before they did anything else, and this was eventually accepted. It was also agreed that the Japanese forces in the Dutch East Indies, Borneo and the Celebes should be bypassed.

The reconquest of the Philippines

Having seized Peleliu in the Palau archipelago and Morotai for their much needed airfields, as well as Ulithi in the Carolines as a fleet anchorage, MacArthur decided to bypass the island of Mindanao and go for Leyte in the center of the Philippines. Landings were made here on October 20, 1944.

The Japanese now tried the same tactic that they had used in the Marianas, that of using their ships to destroy the US ships supporting the landings. Between October 23-26, the Japanese naval forces engaged in battle with the US 3rd and 7th Fleets at Leyte Gulf. The result was a disaster for the Japanese and the destruction of their naval power. They lost no less than four carriers, three battleships, ten cruisers and eleven destroyers. It cost the Americans an aircraft carrier and five smaller ships.

Indicative of the growing Japanese desperation, was the introduction of the *kamikaze* pilot. The word means "divine wind" and the pilots were volunteers for special suicide units which would fly their aircraft, packed with explosives, into Allied ships in the belief that to die for the emperor was the highest form of honor.

The Americans, however, were not to know at the time the extent of the damage which they had inflicted on the Japanese Navy at the Battle of Leyte Gulf. In the meantime, with the Japanese using every form of maritime transport available to reinforce Leyte, the Americans were still locked in combat on the island at the year's end.

The Soviet advance into Poland

The good progress which the Soviets had made during the early months of 1944 on the Eastern Front was maintained during the rest of the year. There was a temporary pause in the spring, but then in May the Russians began to attack once more. In the extreme north they put pressure on Finland. After the relief of Leningrad in January 1944, the Finns had approached the Soviets for an armistice, since they were now isolated from the main German front.

The Soviet terms had been moderate – a return to the agreement of March 1940 – but there was a demand that the Finns disarm the German troops in the north of the country. The Finns could not agree to this. Negotiations were therefore broken off, but in June they were re-opened. Stalin now wanted a formal surrender, but the Finns objected. At the same time, the Germans promised them reinforcements and Finland remained in the war. It was only at this stage that the United States broke off relations with Finland.

Two weeks after the Western Allies had landed in France, the main Soviet offensive resumed. They struck first north of the Pripet Marshes, the one area where the Germans still had a toehold in Soviet territory. Minsk and then Grodno were recaptured, much of northeast Poland was cleared and the German Army Group Center virtually destroyed. The Soviets now attacked south of the Pripet Marshes and soon linked up with the more northern thrust, and at the end of July had closed up to the Vistula, while near the Baltic the German Army Group North was in danger of being cut off in the Courland peninsula. Attention now turned to Warsaw.

The Warsaw Uprising

The Poles had organized an underground army, called the Home Army, under General Tadeusz Bor-Komorowski. When the Germans seemed on the point of evacuating the city, the Polish government in London ordered the Home Army to rise against them. The Poles assumed that the Soviets, who had reached the suburbs of the city, would come to their support. On August 1 the uprising began, but the Soviets made no move to help the Poles.

The Germans rushed reinforcements into the city and for the next two months there was bloody fighting during which much of Warsaw was destroyed. British, American and Free Polish pilots dropped some supplies to the Home Army, but were not allowed to land in Soviet territory, while the Russians themselves began a belated air supply operation in September, but by then it was too late and the Germans crushed all resistance by October 2.

Controversy surrounds the Warsaw Uprising to this day. The Soviets had good military reasons for not getting involved, in that German resistance had been stiffening and their supply lines were very stretched. However, it was not in Stalin's interest to allow Poles directed from London to play a major part in the liberation of their country since it would make Poland more difficult to control after the war.

If the Soviet offensive in the center had come to a halt, this was not so in the South. Beginning on August 20, the Soviets advanced no less than 725 km (450 miles) in 18 days. Rumania quickly surrendered and indeed changed sides, while the Bulgarians, who up until now had managed to retain a semblance of neutrality, made overtures to the British and the United States. The Soviets countered this by invading Bulgaria, which quickly declared war on Germany. The Bulgarians offered no resistance to the Soviet troops, who also occupied the Rumanian oilfields at Ploesti.

The Russians now began a huge outflanking operation designed to roll back the German right flank. They liberated Belgrade, the Yugoslav capital, with the help of Tito's partisans and entered the plains of Hungary. Coming up against Budapest, the Hungarian capital, at the beginning of November, they found the resistance unexpectedly tough and could make no progress. Efforts to outflank the city to the north and south were also checked and by the end of the year Budapest was still in German hands.

German troops, including members of the Waffen-SS, help to crush the Warsaw Uprising, August 1944.

The Germans prepare a counterattack

After the failure of Market Garden, Montgomery had turned his attention to clearing the banks of the Scheldt River, which had to be done if Antwerp was to be used as a port. This was seen as vital to support the Allied advance into Germany. It was finally opened to shipping at the end of November 1944. Leaving the Germans in northern Holland to their own devices, Montgomery gradually reached the German border.

To the south, the US and Free French were doing the same, and the first Allied troops actually crossed the German border in September, near Aachen. There General Courtney Hodges' US First Army became engaged in a very stiff battle in the Hurtgen Forest.

Although the Germans were putting up stiff resistance all along the front, the Western Allies remained confident that it could only be a matter of time before the Germans were finally defeated, especially since, hemmed in on all sides, they were running desperately short of resources with which to prolong the fighting. This optimism was now to be dented.

In great secrecy, Hitler had been planning a counteroffensive in the West designed to recapture Antwerp, thus cutting the Allied supply line as well as splitting the British from the Americans. He chose to mount it through the Ardennes, the same attack route that had proved so successful in May 1940. This time there were, however, differences. For a start it was winter rather than spring, and there was snow and ice on the ground. The Germans did not have their air superiority of 1940 and they were faced by a battle-hardened and confident enemy.

The Germans had three advantages, however. The Allies chose to ignore various pieces of intelligence pointing to a German attack, not believing that they were capable of it. In the event, the Germans were able to assemble an entire army group, including 1,000 tanks, in complete secrecy. The US troops in the Ardennes were either fresh divisions from the United States or licking their wounds after combat in the Hurtgen Forest. Finally, fog masked German movements and placed severe restrictions on Allied air power.

The Battle of the Bulge

The Germans launched their attack on December 16. On the flanks of the attack they were soon held up, but in the center they advanced rapidly, capturing a number of prisoners and creating much confusion. Germans dressed

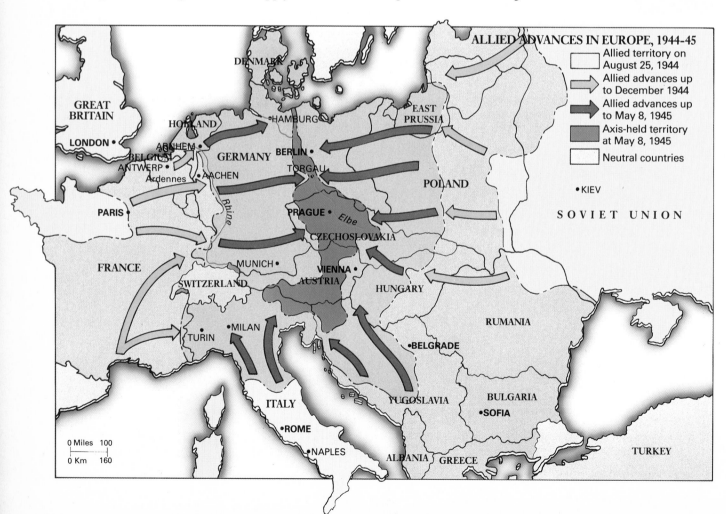

ALLIED ADVANCES IN EUROPE, 1944-45

- Allied territory on August 25, 1944
- Allied advances up to December 1944
- Allied advances up to May 8, 1945
- Axis-held territory at May 8, 1945
- Neutral countries

American troops during Battle of the Bulge.

The Yalta Conference

It would take the Western Allies all of January to recover and begin to advance once more. In the East, the Soviets resumed their offensive on January 12, finally liberating Warsaw five days later. It was against this background of progress in the East but standstill in the West that the three major Allied war leaders, Churchill, Roosevelt and Stalin, met once more, this time at Yalta on the Black Sea.

Victory against Germany was now in sight, and Roosevelt was very keen that the Soviets should become actively involved in the war against Japan. Stalin agreed to declare war as soon as he could after Germany had been defeated. In return, Roosevelt and Churchill gave Stalin a free hand in Poland, Hungary, Rumania and Bulgaria, although there was an assumption that the postwar government of these countries would be determined on the basis of free elections.

Stalin did, however, concede that Greece, where the British were now trying to prevent a takeover by the Communists, would remain in the Western Allies' sphere of influence. In Germany, the Soviets were to be responsible for taking Berlin, since they were much closer to it than the Western Allies. The latter would support the current Soviet offensive by bombing the major cities in the eastern part of Germany.

in American uniforms were sent in to operate behind the lines.

One town, Bastogne, a key communications center in the region, was, however, denied to them. Hastily reinforced by an airborne division, the garrison held tight, allowing the Germans to bypass it but becoming a thorn in the side of the advance.

Furthermore, the Germans were beginning to run very short of fuel, having failed to capture any Allied supplies, something on which they had relied in their planning. Moreover, on December 23, the weather cleared and Allied aircraft were able to support the ground forces. Eisenhower agreed that Montgomery should take command of the northern flank of the salient and he moved British formations forward into blocking positions.

In the south, Patton, seeing what was happening, "read" the battle well and began to plan for a move north even before being given orders to do so. He was thus able to turn his army north in just 48 hours and the relief of Bastogne on December 26 marked the end of German hopes. The Battle of the Bulge was Hitler's last gamble in the west and it had failed.

The bombing of Dresden

With Warsaw captured, the Soviets quickly overran the remainder of Poland, East Prussia was isolated and the Germans were driven back to the line of the Oder and Neisse Rivers. Budapest continued to hold out for some time, and indeed the Germans launched a strong armored counteroffensive in order to relieve the garrison. When this petered out, the garrison finally surrendered on February 13.

That night, February 13, saw one of the more controversial Allied actions of the war, when the RAF bombed Dresden. This was one of the "cities of the east" which the Western Allies had agreed to bomb, but, apart from having many old and historic buildings, it was packed with refugees fleeing from the East. Many have condemned the bombing as inhumane since the city contained no targets of military significance.

Yet it was an attempt to demonstrate to the Germans that the Soviets and the Western Allies were acting together. The Germans rushed troops from the West and were able to halt the Soviet offensive, at least temporarily, by the third week in February.

The Allied advance into Germany

This reduction in German strength in the West helped the Allies to get moving forward once more. The German defenses west of the Rhine quickly collapsed, and they destroyed all the bridges over the river, apart from one at Remagen, which was quickly seized by the Americans. Two weeks later, on March 23 and 24, the British and Americans crossed the Rhine in strength and quickly enveloped and surrounded the Ruhr, taking the surrender of no less than 320,000 German troops trapped there by April 18. The euphoria was dampened, however, by the death of President Roosevelt on April 12, although Vice-President Harry Truman immediately stepped into his place.

Some of Eisenhower's subordinate commanders, notably Montgomery and Patton, wanted him to go direct for Berlin in order to beat the Russians to the city. Eisenhower refused on the grounds that it had already been agreed that Berlin was a Soviet objective.

During the last few months of the war, Hitler's grip on reality faded. Along with his staff, he had installed himself in an underground bunker in Berlin, and seldom appeared above ground. By mid-April the Soviets were advancing once more and had reached the suburbs of Berlin.

In Italy, too, the German defenses were crumbling. After slowly pushing the enemy back during the last half of 1944, the Allies had paused for the winter and then, in April 1945, launched what would turn out to be their final offensive, driving the Germans back toward the passes of the Alps. More and more Italian partisans joined in to harry them in the rear. They also captured Mussolini, who was hiding in the Como area, and unceremoniously shot both him and his mistress, hanging their bodies upside down in a market square. This occurred on April 28, only two days before Hitler took his own life. Later that day, April 30, Russian soldiers hoisted a Soviet flag on top of the ruins of the *Reichstag*, the German parliament.

The German surrender

In the North, the British captured Hamburg and Lübeck, and the Americans reached the Elbe, where they met Soviet troops. Hitler had appointed Admiral Doenitz as his successor. He fled to Schleswig-Holstein, where he negotiated surrender with the Allies. The German forces in Italy had, however, already surrendered unconditionally on April 29, and all fighting finished on May 2. The surrender of all other German forces was signed at Eisenhower's headquarters at Reims.

US troops battling through Germany, 1945.

Churchill and Truman now declared that the war in Europe would formally end the following day, May 8. Stalin was not happy about this, since he had wanted the surrender document signed in Berlin, and he was also keen to capture Prague, capital of Czechoslovakia, before the war's end. It was not until the evening of the 8th that the Soviets informed the Germans still fighting against them that they were to surrender. There was no reply and in the early hours of the following day, after a massive bombardment, Soviet troops entered Prague. Only then did the guns in Europe stop firing.

The war against Japan

This left Japan as a major problem for the Western Allies, since the Soviet Union had still not declared war against her. Troops, aircraft and ships were now transferred from the European theater to the Far East and, indeed, the British already had a fleet operating in the Pacific under the Americans.

Japan was now in a desperate state. Her naval and air power were virtually destroyed. Allied submarines had succeeded in establishing an almost total blockade around the Japanese mainland, which meant that she was now starved of the raw materials, especially rubber and oil, on which she relied to wage war. Furthermore, the Americans had, since November 1944, been bombing the industrial cities of Japan from their bases in the Marianas.

Japanese defeat in Burma

In Burma, the Chinese had continued their advance from the north during the last few months of 1944. In November, at the end of the monsoon (rainy) season, the British had crossed the Chindwin and were driving toward Mandalay. In the Arakan another offensive had been launched. Akyab was seized by amphibious assault in early January 1945, and at the end of the month a determined Japanese counterattack was repulsed at Kangaw.

This offensive slowed down, however, because priority for supplies was switched to the advance on Rangoon. Mandalay fell in March after twelve days' fierce fighting and by the beginning of May the British were at Pegu, only 80 km (50 miles) short of Rangoon. The monsoon broke, but General Slim was, nonetheless, determined to continue his advance.

Troops were landed to the south of Rangoon by sea, and the city itself was secured on May 3. Meanwhile, the Americans were already looking to and tackling their next objectives, designed to take them even closer to the Japanese mainland.

Iwo Jima and Okinawa

The first of these was the island of Iwo Jima, a tiny volcanic island lying 640 km (400 miles) north of the Marianas. The Americans thought it would be a useful base for fighters escorting heavy bombers in raids on Japan. After intensive sea and air bombardment, the US Marines landed on February 19. They expected to secure the island in four days, but such was the ferocity of the Japanese defense, that it took about five weeks and cost the lives of 6,800 Americans.

Okinawa was the next objective. It lies midway between Formosa and Japan, as well as being close to China. It was seen as an ideal base for the invasion of Japan. The Japanese were in considerable strength on the island and had prepared very strong defenses, so the invading forces landing on April 1, found it tough going. *Kamikaze* attacks on the supporting ships led to thirteen being sunk or damaged during the first few days. On April 6, in a final naval flourish, the Japanese sent their last remaining fully operational battleship, *Yamato*, in a suicide attack against the Allied shipping, but she was sunk by US carrier-based aircraft on the next day.

US flamethrower in action during fierce fighting to take Iwo Jima, February 1945.

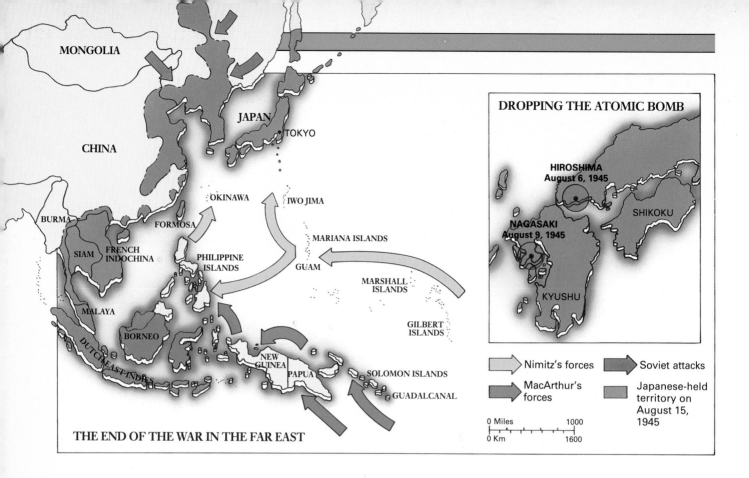

MONGOLIA

CHINA

JAPAN

TOKYO

OKINAWA

IWO JIMA

BURMA

FORMOSA

MARIANA ISLANDS

SIAM

FRENCH
INDOCHINA

PHILIPPINE
ISLANDS

GUAM

MARSHALL
ISLANDS

MALAYA

BORNEO

DUTCH EAST INDIES

NEW
GUINEA

PAPUA

SOLOMON ISLANDS

GUADALCANAL

GILBERT
ISLANDS

THE END OF THE WAR IN THE FAR EAST

DROPPING THE ATOMIC BOMB

HIROSHIMA
August 6, 1945

SHIKOKU

NAGASAKI
August 9, 1945

KYUSHU

Nimitz's forces

Soviet attacks

MacArthur's
forces

Japanese-held
territory on
August 15,
1945

0 Miles   1000
0 Km   1600

In the end, it took three months to clear Okinawa, and the campaign cost the Americans some 50,000 casualties (12,500 killed) and the Japanese 110,000. It seemed that the closer the Allies got to the Japanese mainland, the more desperate and fanatical the Japanese resistance became. They viewed the invasion of Japan itself with increasing concern.

The US Army Air Force maintained the bombing offensive against Japan, sending Boeing B-29 bombers on daytime raids. When these proved disappointingly ineffective, nighttime fire raids were started. The most spectacular of these was on March 9-10 when 234 B-29s dropped over 1,700 tons of incendiary bombs on Tokyo, starting fires in 40 per cent of the capital and killing 80,000 people. These raids ruined the war economy and shook civilian morale.

Potsdam Conference

In mid-July 1945 the last of the great Allied wartime conferences took place at Potsdam, a suburb of Berlin. Attending were President Truman, Stalin and Churchill. Apart from agreeing that the government of Germany would rest in the hands of the four major powers – Britain, France, the United States and the Soviet Union – each of whom would have a zone of occupation, and that the seat of government would be in Berlin, the main topic on the agenda was how to hasten the defeat of Japan.

The Potsdam Conference was dominated by the fact that the United States had at last developed the atomic bomb. Indeed, the first was exploded as a test on July 16. This gave the United States the means to bring the war against Japan to a quick end as well as an advantage in dealing with increasing Soviet stubbornness on the future of the postwar world.

Some of Truman's circle of military advisers did not consider it necessary to use the atomic bomb on Japan. They believed that the unceasing air attacks on the Japanese mainland, combined with the destruction of her naval power and her virtually complete lack of the necessary raw materials with which to continue the war, meant that she was already beaten. Even without an Allied invasion, it was merely a matter of time before she would surrender. Furthermore, the Japanese had been putting out peace feelers and the only sticking point appeared to be the question of unconditional surrender: the Potsdam declaration demanded that Japan be occupied and its war criminals tried. A Soviet declaration of war might well make this a problem of little consequence.

On the other hand, there were indications that the Japanese government was not speaking with one voice and it was known that it included a sizeable militarist element that was prepared to fight on regardless of the cost. If this faction gained the upper hand, then invasion might well become necessary.

Dropping the atomic bomb

Having obtained Stalin's agreement that he would finally declare war on Japan, Truman told him that the United States now possessed a more powerful bomb than any previously used. This was the atomic bomb which Stalin may have known about from Soviet spies in the United States. On July 26, Truman, Churchill and Chiang Kai-shek issued a joint ultimatum to Japan demanding unconditional surrender.

The Japanese government did not respond in any positive way to begin with, and Truman ordered that the bomb be used as soon as possible after August 2. On that very same day, the Japanese ambassador to Moscow, on the instructions of his government, asked the Soviet government to negotiate with the Western Allies on Japan's behalf, but the Soviet foreign minister, Vyacheslav Molotov, refused to see him until August 8, when the Soviet Union declared war.

In the meantime, in the early hours of August 6, a B-29 called *Enola Gay* took off from Tinian, in the Marianas, carrying the first operational atomic bomb. Its target was the city of Hiroshima. At 8:15 A.M. local time the bomb was dropped and the explosion killed 80,000 people outright, seriously injured 37,000, obliterated over 6,325 hectares (4 square miles) and caused complete chaos.

The Japanese government faced an intense debate between those who wanted to surrender immediately and those who wished to continue fighting until the end. The only area of agreement was that the institution of the emperor must be maintained. With no immediate reaction forthcoming, the Americans dropped a second bomb, this time on Nagasaki, on August 9. That same day, the Soviets launched a massive attack on the Japanese forces in Manchuria.

The Japanese surrender

The shock of these three events caused Emperor Hirohito to do something that no Japanese emperor had ever done before. On the next day, the 10th, he spoke at a Cabinet meeting, siding with the peace party in order to save his people further suffering. Messages were sent expressing the Japanese willingness to surrender, but it was to be another four days and a further intercession by the emperor before the unconditional surrender was finally accepted. The emperor announced the surrender on the radio to his people in another unprecedented step. Only, however, with the formal surrender ceremony presided over by General MacArthur on board the battleship USS *Missouri* on September 2, 1945, could the Second World War finally be said to have ended.

The aftermath of the B-29 fire raids: devastation in Tokyo, 1945.

Belsen: the horror of the concentration camps.

CHAPTER 4
THE IMPACT OF WAR

The Second World War, far more than its predecessor, revealed the true horrors of total war, with civilians finding themselves time and again on the front line. It left Europe and many other parts of the world physically and economically exhausted and ill-equipped to face the problems of the postwar world. The human cost had been catastrophic, and the survivors – among them millions of refugees and shattered families – faced the task of reconstruction in the midst of economic chaos, food shortages, black markets and ruined cities. New political arrangements were needed to restore order to the defeated and formerly occupied countries. At the same time, the old colonial empires had been fatally weakened, and confrontations between the United States and the Soviet Union carried the threat of future nightmares. In 1945, hopes that the world could resolve its current and future problems without recourse to conflict now lay in the United Nations.

During the six years of the Second World War no less than 50 million people lost their lives. It was the most costly war, in terms of human life, in history. Yet, of these, less than 17 million were combatants, almost the same total as in the First World War. The Soviet Union suffered the highest casualties, with 20 million deaths, but Poland, where the war had begun, suffered most, with some 22 per cent of her population being killed. The high proportion of civilian casualties meant that it was truly a total war, and there were few parts of the world where its effects were not felt.

As in any war, the Second World War brought out both "man's inhumanity to man" and the highest qualities of humankind. The atrocities which took place in the German concentration camps and Japanese prisoner-of-war camps illustrated only too well how cruel humans can be. On the other hand, the countless acts of selfless bravery and sacrifice on the battlefield, in the concentration camps, during the bombing of cities and elsewhere showed the best of human nature.

The horror of war affected both rich and poor equally. This helped break down class barriers in the democracies of Western Europe, which was reflected in the election of Socialist governments to power in the immediate aftermath.

The US was never directly attacked and her people did not suffer the same hardship as elsewhere. Being self-sufficient in food, neither Canadians nor Americans were subjected to the same stringent food rationing that Europeans had to endure.

The contribution of women and blacks

In the United States, as in Europe, there was conscription and this meant not just finding manpower for the armed forces, but also for the factories producing war materials. This affected women as well as men, with only mothers of small children being exempted. In many countries, women had done some form of war work, either in uniform or in the factories and elsewhere, to allow men to fight during 1914-18, but it was on a greater scale in the Second World War.

Only in the Soviet Union, however, did women serve on the front line and actually kill the enemy. There was a bomber regiment composed entirely of women pilots, which greatly distinguished itself, and during the fighting for Stalingrad at least one female sniper was made a Hero of the Soviet Union, Russia's highest award. In other countries women also came very close to killing. In Britain, for instance, it was more often than not a woman who located approaching German bombers and another woman who directed the anti-aircraft guns onto them. However, she was not allowed to pull the trigger.

Women proved to be as brave as men. Some of the greatest names in the various resistance movements in the occupied countries in Europe were of women, and the women partisans in Yugoslavia suffered exactly the same hardships as their male counterparts. Thus women took another stride forward in their battle to establish equality with men, although, as after 1918, they lost ground as men came back from the war and reclaimed the jobs that they felt were traditionally the male preserve.

Within the US Armed Forces, segregation between blacks and whites was maintained, and the only difference from 1917-18 was that black units were given a combat role. It would take another war, in Korea, before segregation was broken down.

The breakup of the British Empire

For the different peoples of the British Empire, the war marked a significant landmark in the struggle for self-determination. This was especially so in Southeast Asia, where the early Japanese victories had demonstrated that the white man was not all-powerful.

The rescue services help out following a V-2 attack in London, March 1945.

While some Indians and Burmese transferred their allegiance to Japan, the concept of the Greater East Asia Co-prosperity Sphere, proposed by the Japanese, did not work. This was mainly due to the often brutal treatment handed out to the inhabitants of Japanese-occupied countries. Nevertheless, those who fought for the British felt that Britain could only repay her debt by granting their countries independence.

Britain's relationship with the Commonwealth also changed. Both Australia and Canada fell more under the influence of the United States. Australia especially had been more closely involved with the United States during the campaign in the Pacific.

Refugee problems

In Western Europe a new breed of people had been created, Displaced Persons. These included the survivors of Hitler's concentration camps, who had lost everything; those who had been press-ganged into working in German factories and fields; those who feared to return to Eastern Europe; those who fought in the free forces of the occupied countries but had no wish to be under Soviet domination; and those foreign nationals who had fought on the German side, voluntarily or otherwise. Above all there were the Jews. Many had no wish to remain in Europe and wanted to settle in Palestine.

The spread of communism

The Soviet Union had suffered greater loss of life than the Western Allies. However, the prospects for the spread of international communism in 1945 were brighter than they had been even in 1919. Eastern Europe was now dominated by Soviet Russia, although she had agreed that the people of these countries would have the right to decide their own form of postwar government through free elections. In the Balkans, Tito was all-powerful in Yugoslavia, and in Albania, too, Communist partisans had the upper hand. In Greece, civil war between Communists and those who looked to the Western democracies continued to flare up, with British troops supporting the latter.

In the Far East, Communist guerrillas had often taken the leading role in operations against the Japanese occupation forces. By the end of the war those in Malaya and Indochina, equipped with arms supplied by the Allies (and captured from the Japanese), were poised to seize power.

Indeed, as early as September 1945, taking advantage of the fact that the Free French were in no position to reestablish themselves in Indochina, Ho Chi Minh declared an independent republic of Vietnam. The struggle against communism in Vietnam would engage the French and then the Americans for the next thirty years. In China, too, Mao Tse-tung was ready to seize power from Chiang Kai-shek.

Economic problems

Perhaps the most serious problem in 1945 was economic. In many countries, industry had been destroyed, people were homeless, food was short. In Germany and Italy this was the result of both fighting on land and the strategic bombing campaign, which had largely destroyed the railways and roads. Thus the Allies had to take total responsibility for the conquered peoples. In Japan, with the government still intact, the situation was not as bad, but the US bombing had virtually destroyed Japanese industry.

The triumph of the Allies: Soviet troops raise the red flag over the German parliament building in Berlin, April 1945.

The Western European countries which had been under German occupation were also in a bad way. They, too, had suffered from the bombing, especially since it had been concentrated on industry and communications, and France and the Low Countries had also been fought over and suffered much damage as a result. Britain was not in a position to shoulder too much of the burden. The enormous cost of the war had left her virtually bankrupt, her people were exhausted, and large parts of her major towns and cities had been devastated.

Only the United States emerged from the war in a stronger position. It was US industry which had provided the hardware and equipment necessary for final victory. The war had stimulated her economy and all the Allied nations were in her debt. During the later wartime Allied conferences, the Americans began to dominate proceedings, especially in dealings with the enigmatic Stalin.

The possession of the atomic bomb also gave the United States an enormous advantage, although whether the Russians realized this was not yet clear. Certainly, President Truman, like President Wilson in 1918, had announced that the United States would shoulder her share of the burdens of the world.

Setting up the United Nations

Another urgent task was to set up some mechanism which could ensure that there would never be another conflict on the scale of 1939-45, especially with the emergence of the atomic bomb. After the First World War, the League of Nations had failed to do this, but there was hope in its successor, the United Nations. On January 1, 1942, twenty-six nations then fighting Germany, including the exiled governments of the occupied countries, had signed a declaration of cooperation in which the term United Nations was first used. Another twenty-one countries later followed suit.

At Tehran on December 1, 1943, Roosevelt, Stalin and Churchill had declared that they recognized the responsibility resting on the United Nations "to make a peace which will command the goodwill of the overwhelming masses of the peoples in the world and banish the terror and scourge of war for many generations."

However, it was not until the late summer and early autumn of 1944 that the structure of the postwar United Nations was set down. This took place at a two-phase Allied conference, held at Dumbarton Oaks in Washington, D.C. This was followed by the San Francisco Conference in the spring and early summer of 1945, attended by the representatives of fifty nations. Out of these meetings the United Nations Charter was produced in detail. On October 24, 1945, the Charter came into force to mark a new step forward in achieving lasting world peace.

The postwar world

The problems facing the world in 1945 were more formidable than those of 1918, even though the extent of victory was much greater. Indeed, in many ways the Second World War had brought to the fore a number of global problems which had been growing before 1939. German, Italian and Japanese fascism had been vanquished, but the war had not solved the conflicts between communism and capitalism, colonialism and self-determination, "haves" and "have nots," Jew and Arab and many others. The post-1945 world was not to be an easy place in which to live.

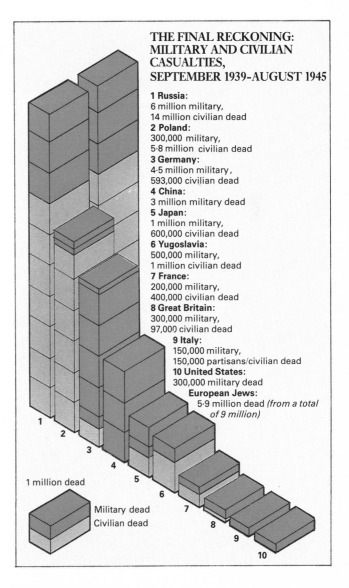

THE FINAL RECKONING: MILITARY AND CIVILIAN CASUALTIES, SEPTEMBER 1939-AUGUST 1945

1 Russia:
6 million military,
14 million civilian dead
2 Poland:
300,000 military,
5·8 million civilian dead
3 Germany:
4·5 million military,
593,000 civilian dead
4 China:
3 million military dead
5 Japan:
1 million military,
600,000 civilian dead
6 Yugoslavia:
500,000 military,
1 million civilian dead
7 France:
200,000 military,
400,000 civilian dead
8 Great Britain:
300,000 military,
97,000 civilian dead
9 Italy:
150,000 military,
150,000 partisans/civilian dead
10 United States:
300,000 military dead
European Jews:
5·9 million dead *(from a total of 9 million)*

1 million dead

Military dead
Civilian dead

CONFLICT IN THE 20TH CENTURY: APPENDICES

The style of warfare between 1939 and 1945 reflected the technological developments in weapons during the previous 20 years. The most successful commanders were those who had the vision to exploit these new weapons to the utmost and the flexibility to adapt them to the varying conditions in each theater of war. Both sides improved and developed ways of fighting in the jungle, desert, at sea and in the air.

THE KEY COMMANDERS

Charles de Gaulle (1890-1970) Free French leader. De Gaulle became the leading exponent of armored warfare in France in the 1930s. In May 1940 he was in command of an armored division and then briefly became Undersecretary of War before fleeing to Britain just before the French armistice with the Germans. He soon became the leader of the Free French and his moment of triumph came in August 1944 when he returned to Paris and was installed as President of the Committee of National Liberation. His single-minded aim to restore French fortunes made him a difficult ally, and he bitterly resented not being invited to the Tehran and Yalta conferences. He was President of France 1945-46 as well as from 1958-69.

Dwight Eisenhower (1890-1969) American general and Supreme Allied Commander in Europe. Eisenhower was a founder member of the US Tank Corps, but did not see action in the First World War. In June 1942, he was appointed commander of US forces in Europe. He was in charge of the Allied operations in North Africa 1942-43 and the invasions of Sicily and Italy. In December 1943 he became Supreme Commander, Allied Expeditionary Force in Europe and as such conducted Overlord and the campaign in Northwest Europe. His powers of diplomacy made him an ideal coalition warfare commander.

He was NATO's first Supreme Allied Commander Europe (1950-52) and President of the United States (1953-61).

Dwight Eisenhower

Heinz Guderian

Heinz Guderian (1888-1954) German Panzer commander. Guderian was appointed General of Panzer Troops in 1938 and played a leading role in the Polish and French campaigns and the invasion of Russia in 1941. Dismissed by Hitler at the end of 1941 for making a tactical withdrawal against orders, he was recalled to duty as Inspector of Panzer Troops in early 1943. He rose to be Chief of Staff of the German Army in July 1944, only to be dismissed in March 1945.

Arthur Harris (1892-1984) British Marshal of the RAF. One of the most controversial figures of the Second World War, "Bomber" Harris led RAF Bomber Command from 1942 until the end of the war. He firmly believed that Germany could be brought to defeat through bombing.

Douglas MacArthur (1880-1964) American general and Allied commander. After a distinguished fighting record in the First World War, MacArthur rose to be Chief of Staff of the US Army and then became military adviser to the government of the Philippines. Recalled to active duty in July 1941, he conducted the defense of the Philippines against the Japanese and then became commander of the Southwest Pacific area. His "island-hopping" strategy was highly successful and saved many casualties. He finished the war as Supreme Commander for the Allied Powers in the Pacific theater. He later commanded the United Nations' forces in the Korean War, but was removed for wanting to extend the war to Red China.

Bernard Montgomery (1887-1976)
British army commander. "Monty"
was one of the few commanders to
come out of the campaign in France
in 1940 with his reputation intact.
Appointed to command the British
Eighth Army in Egypt in August
1942, he led it through North Africa,
Sicily and Italy and then from 1944
commanded 21st Army Group in the
Normandy landings and in Northwest Europe. The secret of his
success was careful preparation for
his battles and ensuring that every
man knew what was expected of
him. His brash self-confidence,
while a morale booster to his own
men, created much friction with his
fellow commanders in the Allied
camp. After the war, he became
Chief of the British General Staff and
then NATO Supreme Allied
Commander Europe.

Chester Nimitz (1885-1966)
American admiral. An outstanding
US naval commander, Nimitz was
given command of the US Pacific
Fleet shortly after Pearl Harbor. His
intelligent use of information
gleaned from intercepts of top secret
Japanese messages resulted in the
victory at Midway and from then on
he commanded the drive toward
Japan in the Central Pacific. He
maintained a rivalry with
MacArthur for resources in the
Pacific. Quiet and efficient, he was
highly regarded by all.

Isoroku Yamamoto

Konstantin Rokossovsky (1896-
1968) Soviet army commander.
Dismissed from the Soviet Army and
imprisoned during Stalin's purges in
the 1930s, Rokossovsky was recalled
during the Russo-Finnish War. He
first made a name for himself in the
defense of Moscow at the end of
1941 and then played a leading role
in the victory at Stalingrad. As
commander of the Belorussian
Front, he failed to go to the help of
the Poles in Warsaw in August 1944.
In 1945 he cleared northern Poland
and Danzig and met with the British
near Lübeck.

Erwin Rommel (1891-1944) German
army commander. Rommel won
Germany's highest bravery award in
the First World War. He proved
himself a skilled tank division
commander in France in 1940. He
took the *Deutsches Afrika Korps* to
Libya in early 1941 and for the next
18 months consistently outfought
the British. After his defeat at El
Alamein he conducted a very skilful
withdrawal into Tunisia, where he
surprised the Americans at
Kasserine Pass. After tours of duty in
Italy and the Balkans, he took charge
of Army Group B in France until
wounded in July 1944. Implicated in
the Bomb Plot, he was forced to take
his own life. A fearless commander,
who led from the front, he was
popular with his men.

Isoroku Yamamoto (1884-1943)
Japanese admiral. Responsible for
building up the Japanese Navy
before the war, Yamamoto was
opposed to going to war with the
United States. Nevertheless he
planned the attack on Pearl Harbor.
Having studied at Harvard
University and been the naval
attaché in the United States, he was
convinced that Japan would lose in
the long run and he believed in
inflicting the greatest possible
damage in the shortest period of time
so that Japan could obtain the best
possible peace terms. He succeeded
at Pearl Harbor, but failed at Midway.
In April 1943 he died when his
aircraft was shot down by US fighters.

Georgi Zhukov (1896-1974) Soviet
military commander. He first came
to prominence during the operations
against the Japanese in Mongolia just
before the outbreak of the Second
World War and was appointed Chief
of Staff of the Soviet Army in
January 1941. Later, in August 1942,
he became Deputy Commissar for
Defense. He was deeply involved in
the overall conduct of all Soviet
operations on the Eastern Front, but
often took personal charge,
especially during the siege of
Leningrad, the 1944 offensives and
the capture of Berlin. At the
beginning of the war, he was
cautious but became more daring
and decisive.

Bernard Montgomery

Georgi Zhukov

WARFARE DEVELOPMENTS

Blitzkrieg

Blitzkrieg means "lightning war" and was the secret of the German success on land during 1939-42. The doctrine was developed by British military theorists Major General J. F. C. Fuller and Captain Basil Liddell Hart, but the Germans, especially General Guderian, applied it in the 1930s.

In essence *Blitzkrieg* meant the paralyzing of the enemy through the use of fast-moving armored columns closely supported by aircraft. These were used as aerial artillery, to slice through the enemy defenses and disrupt their ability to command and control their forces. Follow-up troops would then reduce the defenses still holding out. It proved remarkably successful in Poland, France and the Balkans.

In Russia, however, *Blitzkrieg* faltered mainly because of the vastness of the country. Also Hitler launched his attack too late in the year, which meant that the tanks ground to a halt in the autumn mud and winter snow. The weather also hampered fuel and fodder supplies (much of the German army still relied on horse-drawn transport). The Allies, too, adopted the *Blitzkrieg* concept, especially after the breakout from Normandy in 1944, and during the Soviet offensives on the Eastern Front in 1944-45.

Jungle warfare

The Japanese victories after Pearl Harbor quickly revealed that the Japanese understood the jungle, while the Allies did not. Indeed, the Allies failed to recognize that jungle fighting meant not just battle tactics, but also learning to live in the jungle, which can be a frightening place for those who do not know it. Gradually, however, spearheaded by the Chindits, Merrill's Marauders and the Australians in New Guinea, the Allies learned to fight as well as their

enemies in the jungle.

It is very easy to outflank and infiltrate defenses in the jungle, so the Allies learned to stand fast rather than withdraw and to disrupt the enemy by frequent counterattacks. Another important tactic was the ambush, for which, of course, the jungle is ideally suited. The troops had to be trained to react very rapidly, especially in returning quick and accurate fire.

Resupply was always a problem, although not so much for the Japanese, who were able to subsist on very little. The Allies, on the other hand, placed increasing emphasis on resupply by air, either dropping supplies by parachute or using makeshift landing strips. Malaria was a constant problem and soldiers had to take tablets daily to protect themselves from it.

Desert warfare

The North African desert was by far the "cleanest" battleground since, apart from wandering Arabs and the coastal towns, there was little chance of large numbers of civilians being caught in the fighting. The dominant weapon was the tank, and the campaign was marked by bursts of fast-moving and furious fighting followed by sometimes long pauses while both sides drew breath and regrouped. Because advances were often rapid, supply lines became very stretched, and for a long time it was this that prevented either side from winning a decisive victory.

For much of the time, Rommel handled his tanks much better than the British. He kept his tank forces concentrated, while the British tended to split theirs up. Often, too, Rommel would lure the British tanks into a trap, using his own armor to draw them toward cunningly concealed anti-tank guns, of which the foremost was the 88 mm.

Another aspect which marked the fighting was the extensive use of

Special Forces by both sides. The main battle area was always close to the coast, but the vastness of the Libyan Desert meant that there was always an open flank, of which both sides, but more especially the British, took advantage. Small teams of men were used to gather intelligence and cause disruption behind the enemy's lines.

Battle of the Atlantic

This was the most crucial campaign of the war at sea. As an island nation, Britain had to maintain her maritime trade, and her transatlantic links were vital, as had been demonstrated by the U-boat campaign in the First World War.

While convoying was instituted by the British in 1939, there was a desperate shortage of escort ships and aircraft. Likewise, although the Germans had only 50 U-boats at the onset, these were soon inflicting damage out of all proportion to their numbers, and surface ships and aircraft also played their part.

Doenitz, the Flag Officer U-boats, convinced Hitler that priority must be given to U-boat construction and soon many more merchant ships were being sunk than could be replaced. In 1940 Doenitz introduced the "wolf pack" concept, which meant groups of U-boats deployed along the convoy routes, notably in the "Black Gap" in the mid-Atlantic which was beyond the range of British and North American air cover.

The fortunes of both sides rose and fell, but in mid-1943 came the turning point when the Allies finally got the upper hand. Their eventual success was due to a number of factors – the ability to decipher radio traffic between the U-boat headquarters and the U-boats at sea, improved technical aids for detecting and destroying U-boats, long-range patrol aircraft and good escort drills.

U-boats under construction, 1941.

Airborne warfare

This was a new form of warfare. The Germans were the first to demonstrate how effective airborne forces could be when on May 10, 1940, a party of glider-borne paratroop engineers captured the Belgian fortress of Eben Emael. This was followed by the capture of Crete by paratroops in May 1941. However, airborne operations were also very costly in transport aircraft, and the Germans mounted few after Crete.

The British also formed parachute battalions, which were used in Tunisia and during the invasion of Sicily. The Normandy landings were preceded by US and British airborne landings. The tragedy at Arnhem in September 1944 showed that airborne troops had to be relieved quickly by ground forces. They did, however, play a crucial role in the British crossings of the Rhine.

Strategic Bombing

Before the war it was thought that the bomber aircraft was invincible and could be used to defeat a state by direct attacks on its centers of government and population. Although there was no formal prohibition of the bombing of civilians, both sides went to war recognizing that such attacks went against the spirit of the laws of war. Apart from the bombing of Warsaw in 1939, which the Germans deemed a military target because the Poles would not surrender, and of Rotterdam, which was bombed by mistake in May 1940, both sides held to this until the Battle of Britain.

The use of radar and the monoplane fighter did, however, prove that the bomber could be intercepted and shot down before it reached its target. The British and Germans were therefore forced to mount their bombing attacks by night in order to protect their aircraft from fighters. Inaccurate bomb-aiming devices and navigation systems meant that bombing accuracy was low and civilian targets were inevitably hit. As a result, both reverted to "area bombing," designed to affect civilian morale and hit war industries.

The Germans failed to bring about the collapse of Britain during the Blitz in the winter of 1940-41. The Allies also failed against Germany, although industry was severely, but not critically, disrupted. The Americans believed that daylight bombing could succeed if bombers were given sufficient protective armament, but their experiences over Germany during 1943 showed that this was not enough and long-range fighter escorts were needed.

Bombing by night became a technological battle. On the one side there was the need to detect and intercept the bomber, and on the other to achieve navigational and homing accuracy, as well as protection against night fighters. It can be said that the dropping of the atomic bombs on Japan reppresented the only decisive use of strategic bombing.

Enola Gay, *the converted B-29 which dropped the atomic bomb on Hiroshima.*

LAND WEAPONS

Tanks

At the outbreak of war, tanks were basically of three types – heavy, medium and light. Heavy tanks were used to break through enemy defenses, medium tanks to exploit a breakthrough and light tanks to carry out the traditional cavalry role of reconnaissance, although this was also done by armored cars. There were, however, exceptions to this general rule in that the Germans had no heavy tanks, since they did not fit into the fast-moving *Blitzkrieg* concept, and neither did the British, who had infantry support tanks instead.

As the war progressed, tank design became very much a race between gun and armor, but there were penalties to be paid. A tank with a big gun and very thick armor was inevitably very large, which meant that its mobility suffered. This was especially so with some of the later German models – the Panther and the Royal Tiger – although they were formidable in defense.

The alternative was to look for a compromise between firepower, mobility and protection. Good examples of this were the US Sherman, the most widely produced tank of the war, the German PzKpfw IV and the Soviet T-34, perhaps the best tank, in terms of robustness and simplicity, to be produced by either side.

There were also, especially by the British, developments in "specialized armor," tanks for particular tasks, such as bridgelayer tanks and tanks fitted with flails for clearing mines.

Some countries produced armored fighting vehicles with the sole task of destroying other tanks. The Americans developed the tank destroyer, the Germans the *Sturmpanzer* and *Jadgpanzer* and the Soviets the SU assault gun.

Artillery

Although the Germans and, to a lesser extent, the British, with their coastal artillery, did carry on the First World War tradition of "super heavy" artillery, the main emphasis during 1939-45 was on mobility. Artillery had to be able to keep up with and support fast-moving armored formations at all times. It was the field gun – the US 105-mm howitzer, British 25 pounder, German 105 mm and Soviet 76 mm – which was the workhorse of both sides, backed up with medium guns of 155-mm caliber.

By the middle of the war, self-propelled artillery, often using an existing tank chassis, began to be introduced to give even greater mobility, and examples of this were the German *Hummel* and the Canadian-designed Sexton. Wheeled antitank guns were also an artillery responsibility and, like tank guns, calibers grew larger as tanks became better protected.

Undoubtedly, the most formidable of these was the German 88 mm, which was feared by all Allied tank crews.

The other main artillery branch was anti-aircraft, and guns ranged from large caliber used against high-flying bombers to small, highly mobile quick-firing cannon like the Swedish-designed Bofors.

A Soviet T-34 tank in action on the Eastern Front.

A US Sherman tank falls into German hands in 1944.

Fig. 2

The German PzKpfw IV　　　　*The German 88-mm antitank gun*

Infantry weapons

The infantryman's basic weapon, the rifle and bayonet, remained much the same as in 1914-18. However, light machine guns weighing much less than their 1914-18 forebears and submachine guns were developed to increase an infantryman's firepower at the lowest level.

Mortars, the infantry's own "artillery," were also much lighter than the cumbersome trench mortars of the First World War.

In fact the greatest concern of the infantry was the tank threat. In 1939, most armies were equipped with the antitank rifle, but this soon became ineffective because of the increasing thickness of tank armor. The solution lay in the hollow charge, or Monro effect, named for the US engineer who discovered it in the 1880s.

A projectile with a cone-like hollow head lined with metal would, when detonated, create a stream of molten metal and hot gases which would penetrate armor. The US Bazooka, German *Panzerfaust* and British Projector Infantry Anti-Tank (PIAT) were all excellent tank-ambush weapons.

Rockets

There were some notable rocket developments during the Second World War. On the battlefield itself it was the appearance of the multiple-barreled rocket launcher, the German *Nebelwerfer* and Soviet *Katyusha*. They were important

because they could put down a heavy weight of explosive onto a small area of ground. Curiously, the Western Allies never adopted this weapon to the same extent except as an amphibious-landing support weapon.

The other major development was in strategic rockets and missiles, which was an area pursued by the Germans alone. During the late 1930s and the first part of the war, they worked on what became known as *Vergeltungswaffen* ("Vengeance" or V-Weapons), which Hitler

regarded as "miracle weapons" designed to turn impending defeat into victory. There were two types, the V-1, which was in effect a pilotless aircraft packed with explosive, and the V-2, a guided rocket. Not until June 1944, just after the Normandy landings, did the Germans begin to use them in action. London and Antwerp suffered most. Apart from giving the Western Allies a scare, there were never enough produced to have any significant impact on the course of the last year of the war.

The V-2 rocket

NAVAL WEAPONS

Aircraft carriers

The most significant development in the war at sea during 1939-45 was that the aircraft carrier superseded the battleship as the most important warship. The effectiveness of aircraft against warships had been demonstrated by the US air theorist General Billy Mitchell in the early 1920s in a series of experiments using ships laid up from the First World War. Except for Germany and the Soviet Union, all the world's major navies possessed aircraft carriers at the outbreak of war. But it was not until the end of 1941 that the potential of the aircraft carrier was demonstrated with the Japanese attack on Pearl Harbor, which was launched from carriers.

From then on, the aircraft carrier dominated the war in the Pacific, giving navies the ability to mount long-range strikes without bringing their fleets within the range of the enemy guns. Smaller carriers also played their part in protecting convoys against the submarine, using their aircraft to seek and destroy. As a result of the increasing dominance of the carrier, the battleship's roles were reduced to carrier protection and shore bombardment.

Submarines

The power of the submarine also increased. At the outbreak of war submarine ranges were much greater than they had been in 1914-18 and they were true ocean-going vessels. In 1939, however, submarines still suffered from a number of drawbacks. They were not able to operate underwater for long because the air inside the vessel became stale and they had to surface to recharge their batteries. In any event, underwater speeds were low. This meant that a submarine only dived when it was getting close to its target or had been discovered.

Another problem from which the German U-boats suffered, especially in the first year of the war, was torpedo unreliability. It was the Germans who took the lead in overcoming these problems. They developed torpedoes which would automatically home in on the target. The first type had a preset zigzag course which increased the chances of hitting a ship in a convoy. Later they introduced an acoustic torpedo which homed in on the noise of a ship's propellers.

Underwater capability was dramatically improved by the introduction of the *Schnorkel*, which meant that the U-boat could "breathe," and the *Walther* Turbine which enabled the submarine to travel at relatively high speeds underwater and very quietly in order to reduce the risk of detection. These developments, however, came too late to restore Germany's fortunes.

Antisubmarine warfare

SONAR, or ASDIC as the British called it, introduced in 1918, detected a submarine underwater by bouncing sound impulses off it. To detect a submarine on the surface, two types of devices were used, apart from visual contact.

Radar at Sea

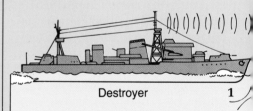

Destroyer   1

SONAR, or ASDIC worked by bouncing sound waves (**1**) off underwater objects such as a submarine (**2**), after which depth-charges (**3**) could be fired to collapse the submarine's hull. On the surface, the submarine (**4**) could be detected by normal radar (**5**), although in this case the target would be smaller.

A US TBF Avenger torpedo bomber flies over aircraft carrier deck.

A Landing Ship Tank, about to unload, southern France, August 1944.

The first was radar, using a rotating aerial, which was operated by hand. By 1943 sets with a 32-km (20-mile) range were in service. Radio direction-finding was the other method. This detected submarine radio transmissions and a bearing to the submarine could be obtained. With two sets operating on different ships, the submarine's exact position could be established by charting the intersection of the bearings.

The top-secret codes used by the German and Japanese submarines, code-named ULTRA and MAGIC respectively, were broken by the Allies at an early stage of the war. They were, as on land and in the air, invaluable in establishing the enemy's intentions, although often the time taken to decipher meant that the information gained was out of date.

To destroy the submarine, the depth charge, delivered by both ships and aircraft, was the main weapon. These were "bombs" fired in a pattern and set to detonate at a certain depth. Later, the British introduced Hedgehog, a launcher which fired 24 explosive projectiles simultaneously, which would only detonate if they hit something solid.

Amphibious warfare

Little attention was paid to landings from the sea before 1939, but they became a very marked characteristic of the Second World War. A successful landing required very close cooperation among air force, navy and army, and it was very important that the troops quickly established themselves on the shore so that they could effectively resist counterattacks.

The most important element of an amphibious landing was the landing craft, flat bottomed with a ramp, which took the troops to the shore. Early types were small and designed merely to land troops, but larger ships were built to carry tanks and other heavy equipment, as well as fire-support vessels armed with guns and multi-barreled rocket launchers.

Often obstacles below the tide line and the nature of the beach meant it was not possible to land troops without getting their feet wet. Kits were developed to enable tanks to swim ashore, as well as special tracked amphibious vehicles, which could also swim.

Mines

As in the First World War, mines played an important part in the war at sea. They were laid by both ships and aircraft. The traditional type of mine, which relied on a ship hitting it to detonate it, quickly gave way to the magnetic type. The answer to this was degaussing. A cable, placed around the hull of the ship and connected to the generators, could produce a countermagnetic field and cancel out the existing one.

Acoustic mines, detonated by the noise of the ship's propellers, and pressure mines, which worked by responding to the varying water pressure under a moving ship, also made their appearance, as did combinations of these. To make the task of rendering them safe more difficult, various anti-handling devices were introduced. Another type of mine was the limpet, which could be attached to the hull of the ship and had a timing device. It was used in Special Forces operations.

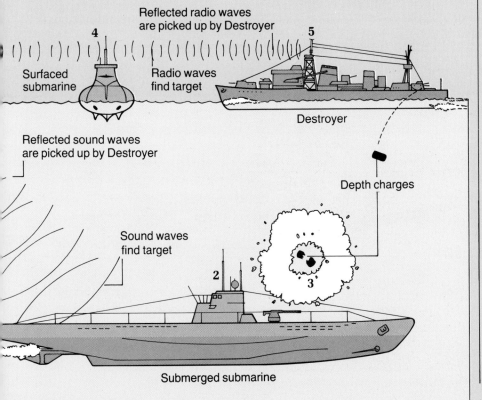

Reflected radio waves are picked up by Destroyer

4

Surfaced submarine

Radio waves find target

5

Destroyer

Reflected sound waves are picked up by Destroyer

Depth charges

Sound waves find target

2

3

Submerged submarine

AIR WEAPONS

Fighters

It was the monoplane eight-gun fighter, together with radar, which disproved the prewar belief that the bomber "would always get through." In 1939, the British and Germans had some outstanding fighters, the Supermarine Spitfire, Hawker Hurricane and Messerschmitt Bf 109, which were all modified to improve speed and range and remained in service throughout the war. The Japanese Zero outclassed all existing Allied fighters in the early days of the war in the Far East. The Germans also introduced the Focke Wulf Fw190.

The Germans used the Junkers Ju 87 Stuka dive bomber to provide close support for troops on the ground. This was even fitted with sirens to frighten the enemy. The Allies had fighter-bombers like the Soviet Ilyushin Il-2 Sturmovik and the British Typhoon.

To combat night bombers, radar-equipped Messerschmitt Bf 110s and de Havilland Mosquitos were introduced, and to protect day bombers, long-range fighters like the Republic P-47 Thunderbolt and North American P-51 Mustang, with a range of 2,090 km (1,300 miles), eventually gave effective cover.

The most radical development was, however, the appearance of the jet fighter. In 1944 it finally came into service in the shape of the Gloster Meteor, which was used to intercept V-1 flying bombs, and the German Messerschmitt Me 262, which, although somewhat unreliable, had several successes during the last year of the war.

Bombers

The Germans lacked a true strategic bomber in terms of range and bomb-load, and this was one of the reasons they failed to win the Battle of Britain and to disrupt Soviet war industry. The RAF and the USAAF,

The German Me 262 jet had a top speed of 869 km/h (540 mph).

on the other hand, had drawn up specifications for long-range four-engined bombers well before the outbreak of war and these made their appearance in 1941. The two best known were the Avro Lancaster and the Boeing B-17.

There was, however, a difference in philosophy. The Americans, unlike the RAF, believed that if the bomber had enough guns, it could operate by day, and the B-17 was known as the Flying Fortress. However, this only became really possible with the introduction of the long-range fighter escort. Also on long flights the B-17's bomb load was restricted.

However, the situation improved with the appearance of the Boeing B-29 Superfortress, which had a range of 4,500 km (2,800 miles) and a bomb load of 5.5 tons. It was this type that dropped the atomic bombs on Hiroshima and Nagasaki.

Bombs

As the war progressed, bombs became larger and heavier. At the beginning the largest was the 500-pounder (227-kg), but soon 455-kg (1,000-lb) and 909-kg (2,000-lb) bombs were developed.

The heaviest conventional bomb

The North American P-51 Mustang

Lancaster S-Sugar of No 467 Squadron is 'bombed up.'

aircraft flying toward England. It was originally called Radiolocation, implying the use of radio waves bounced off solid objects, but the US name of Radar (*Radio Direction and Ranging*) was soon universally adopted. Radar played a vital role in the Battle of Britain, and the Germans soon afterward set up their own system, combined with antiaircraft guns and night fighters, to protect Germany from the RAF's night bombing.

This was called the Kammhuber Line after the general responsible for installing it. Radars installed in night fighters enabled them to detect, locate and attack enemy bombers. Likewise, the bombers themselves had radar systems which enabled them to locate their targets accurately.

Systems were also introduced to jam or confuse the enemy's radars. The best known was Window, which consisted of strips of aluminum which were dropped by the bombers, producing a cloud-like effect on the radar's display. This system, now called Chaff, is still very much in use as a counter to missile attack.

of all was the British 9,975-kg (22,000-lb) Grand Slam, which was used to destroy the Bielefeld railway viaduct in Germany in March 1945. Incendiary bombs, using thermite or phosphorus, and delayed action bombs were also used by both sides.

The most awesome and revolutionary development was the atomic bomb. At the beginning of the war scientists began to investigate how atomic energy could be transformed into a weapon. With the entry of the United States into the war, all Allied efforts were pooled in the United States under what was called the Manhattan Project. It was not until July 16, 1945 that an atomic bomb was successfully test-exploded, at Alamogordo in the New Mexico desert.

Radar

Radar came to dominate the war in the air, perhaps even more so than at sea. It was the British who first installed a defensive system in the late 1930s in order to detect hostile

British Chain Home Radar, 1940

Coastal radar (**1**) picks up bombers (**2**); information is fed back (**3**) to fighters (**4**).

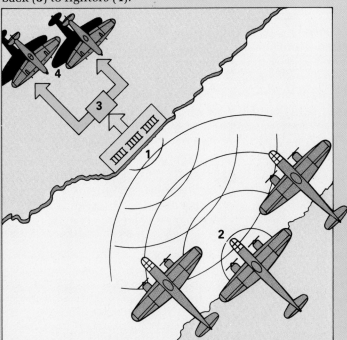

"Window" at War, 1944

Lead aircraft (**1**) drops "Window" (**2**) to confuse radars (**3**) and protect bombers (**4**).

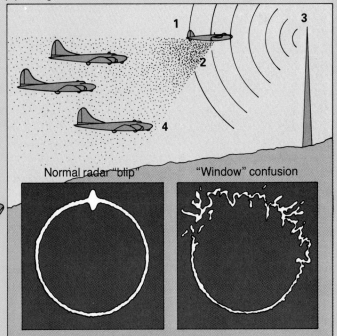

Normal radar "blip"   "Window" confusion

CHRONOLOGY

1939

September 1 German invasion of Poland

September 3 Britain and France declare war on Germany

September 17 Soviet invasion of Poland

November 30 Soviet attack on Finland

1940

March 12 Peace between Soviet Union and Finland signed in Moscow

April 9 German invasion of Denmark and Norway

May 10 German invasion of France and the Low Countries begins; Churchill appointed British prime minister

May 15 Holland surrenders

May 27 Dunkirk evacuation begins

May 28 Belgium surrenders

June 10 Italy declares war, invading southern France next day

June 22 French sign armistice with the Germans

July 3-8 British bombard the French fleet in North African ports

July 16 Hitler issues orders for the invasion of Britain

September 13 Italian forces invade Egypt from Libya

September 15 Climax of the Battle of Britain: London is heavily bombed

September 27 Japan joins Axis

October 7 German troops enter Rumania

October 28 Italy invades Greece from Albania

November 5 Roosevelt reelected US President

November 20 Hungary and then Rumania join the Axis

December 9 British troops begin to drive the Italians out of Egypt

1941

January 19 British invade Eritrea

February 7 Italians decisively defeated at Beda Fomm in Libya

February 8 Germany and Bulgaria sign military pact

March 9 Italy attacks Greece from Albania

March 11 US Lend-Lease Bill becomes law

March 16 British launch recapture of British Somaliland and enter Ethiopia

March 24 Rommel begins his first offensive in Libya

April 6 Germany invades Yugoslavia (surrenders April 17) and Greece (surrenders April 21)

April 13 Soviet Union and Japan sign five-year nonaggression pact

April 29 Pro-Fascist revolt in Iraq, which British put down

May 5 Emperor Haile Selassie re-enters his capital in Ethiopia

May 20 German airborne assault on Crete, which falls on May 31

June 8 British attack Syria

June 22 Hitler invades Soviet Union

July 12 Britain and Soviet Union sign mutual assistance pact

August 9-12 Churchill and Roosevelt meet off Newfoundland and draw up the Atlantic Charter

August 25 British and Soviet troops enter Iran to secure the oilfields

September 8 Leningrad surrounded

November 18 British launch a major offensive in Libya

December 4 German drive on Moscow halted

December 7 Japanese attack on Pearl Harbor brings the United States into the war

December 11 Germany and Italy declare war on the United States

December 22 Churchill and Roosevelt meet in Washington, DC (Arcadia)

December 31 Japanese capture Manila, capital of the Philippines

1942

January 1 26 nations sign the Declaration of the United Nations in Washington, DC

January 6 Axis forces cleared from Cyrenaica (Libya)

January 21 Rommel attacks in Libya

January 31 British cleared from Malaya

February 15 Singapore surrenders

March 7 Japanese enter Rangoon, capital of Burma

April 18 Doolittle raid on Tokyo

May 4-8 Battle of the Coral Sea in the Pacific

May 6 US fortress of Corregidor (Philippines) surrenders

May 19-28 Germans victorious at Kharkov on the Eastern Front

May 26 Rommel attacks and soon breaks the British Gazala Line in Libya

June 4-7 Battle of Midway (Pacific)

June 24 Eisenhower assumes command of all US troops in Europe

July 1-27 First Battle of El Alamein in Egypt

July 3 Germans secure Sevastapol in the Crimea

August 7 US landings on Guadalcanal (Solomon Islands, Pacific)

August 9 Germans capture Caucasus oilfields

August 12 Churchill, Stalin, US and Free French representatives meet in Moscow to discuss the Second Front

August 19 Canadian raid on Dieppe fails

August 30-September 2 Montgomery repulses Rommel at Alam Halfa, Egypt

September 1 Germans reach the outskirts of Stalingrad

October 23-November 4 Second Battle of El Alamein

November 8 Allied landings in French North Africa (Torch)

November 11 Germans occupy Vichy France

November 19 Soviet counter-offensive at Stalingrad

1943

January 14-23 Anglo-US conference at Casablanca

January 31 Germans at Stalingrad surrender

February 9 US troops finally secure Guadalcanal in the Solomons

February 14-22 Battle of Kasserine, Tunisia

April 23 Anglo-US HQ set up in Britain to begin planning the invasion of Europe

May 13 Final surrender of Axis forces in Tunisia

May 16-17 RAF Dambuster raid

May 24 German U-boats ordered temporarily away from North Atlantic

June 21 US Marines land on New Georgia, Solomons

July 5-12 Battle of Kursk (Eastern Front)

July 10 Anglo-US landings in Sicily

July 25 Mussolini overthrown in Italy

July 25-August 3 Hamburg devastated in bombing raids

August 14-24 Allied Quadrant Conference in Quebec

August 17 USAAF lose 60 aircraft in first Schweinfurt raid

August 23 Soviets recapture Kharkov

September 3 Allied landings across the Strait of Messina on Italy

September 8 Italy makes peace with the Allies

September 9 Allied landings at Salerno (Italy)

September 24 Soviets retake Smolensk

October 13 Italy declares war on Germany

October 14 USAAF lose heavily in second Schweinfurt raid

November 6 Soviets retake Kiev

November 20 US landings on Tarawa and Makin in the Gilbert Islands (Pacific)

November 28-December 1 Tehran Conference – Churchill, Roosevelt and Stalin meet

1944

January 22 Allied landings at Anzio, Italy

January 27 Leningrad relieved

January 31 US landings on the Marshall Islands (Pacific)

February 15 Soviets reenter Estonia

February 29 US landings on the Admiralty Islands (Pacific)

March 8 Major Japanese offensive launched in central Burma

March 29 Soviet troops enter Rumania

May 18 Monte Cassino (Italy) captured

June 4 Rome liberated

June 6 Anglo-US landings in Normandy

June 15 US forces land on Saipan (Mariana Islands)

June 19-20 Battle of the Philippine Sea (Pacific)

June 22 Soviet offensive in Belorussia begins

July 9 German Army Group North cut off in the Baltic states

July 20 Attempt on Hitler's life fails

July 25 US troops begin to break out of Normandy beachhead

July 28 Soviets retake Brest-Litovsk

August 1 Polish patriots rise in Warsaw (crushed October 2)

August 15 Allied landings in southern France

August 23 Rumania surrenders to the Soviet Union

August 25 Paris liberated; Allied troops begin attacks on the Gothic Line (Italy)

September 3 Brussels liberated

September 8 Bulgaria declares war on Germany

September 15 US troops cross the German border between Aachen and Luxemburg

September 17-24 Allied airborne operation to seize river crossings in Holland (Market Garden)

September 19 Armistice signed between Finland and the Allies

October 20 US landings, Leyte

October 23-26 Battle of Leyte Gulf off the Philippines

November 7 President Roosevelt elected for a fourth term

December 15 US landings on Mindoro in the Philippines

December 16-January 20, 1945 German counteroffensive in the Ardennes (Battle of the Bulge)

1945

January 17 Warsaw liberated

February 4-11 Yalta Conference with Churchill, Roosevelt and Stalin

February 13 Budapest finally falls

February 13-14 Bombing of Dresden

February 19 US landings on Iwo Jima, Pacific

March 3 Manila secured

March 7 US troops seize Remagen bridge over the Rhine

March 9-10 Fire raid on Tokyo

April 1 Final offensive launched in Italy; US landings on Okinawa

April 12 President Roosevelt dies and is succeeded by Truman

April 25 US troops make contact with the Soviets on the Elbe River, southwest of Berlin

April 28 Mussolini killed by partisans

April 29 German forces sign an armistice in Italy

April 30 Hitler commits suicide

May 1 Berlin surrenders to the Soviets

May 3 Rangoon recaptured by the British

May 7 Germany formally surrenders

June 21 Okinawa finally secured

July 16 First successful atomic bomb test

July 16-August 2 Potsdam Conference

July 26 Attlee replaces Churchill as British prime minister

August 6 Atomic bomb dropped on Hiroshima

August 8 Soviet Union declares war on Japan

August 9 Atomic bomb dropped on Nagasaki

September 2 Japan formally surrenders

INDEX

Note: Numbers in bold refer to illustrations or maps